TABLE OF C

―――⟫•◦•⟪―――

Unless otherwise indicated, all Scripture quotations are taken from the King
James Version of the Bible.
The Uncommon Achiever
ISBN 1-56394-150-3/B-133
Copyright © 2007 by **MIKE MURDOCK**
All publishing rights belong exclusively to Wisdom International
Publisher/Editor: Deborah Murdock Johnson
Published by The Wisdom Center · 4051 Denton Hwy. · Ft. Worth, Texas 76117
1-817-759-BOOK · 1-817-759-0300
You Will Love Our Website...! TheWisdomCenter.tv

Accuracy Department: To our Friends and Partners...We welcome any comments
on errors or misprints you find in our book...Email our department:
AccuracyDept@thewisdomcenter.tv. Your aid in helping us excel is highly valued.

Decisiveness Is Magnetic.

-MIKE MURDOCK

≈ 1 ≈

DISTINGUISH BETWEEN WHAT MATTERS AND WHAT DOES NOT

Be Decisive.

Few people are.

Have you ever noticed the *hesitation* in drivers at a four-way stop? I have seen people sit for thirty seconds at a four-way stop waiting for everyone else to make the first move! I have sat at restaurants with people who could not decide in twenty minutes what food they wanted to eat! Some have even asked the waitress what she thought they should eat!

Develop decisiveness. *Think* about what you want. Give it *thought.* Invest the Seed of time. *Contemplate. Meditate* on it.

What do you want to be happening in the circle of your life ten years from today? What are the *ideal* circumstances for your retirement? *What do you dream of becoming?* Do you have a personal list of goals and dreams? Have you taken the time to write them out in detail?

Several years ago, a brilliant young lady suggested that I take a tape recorder, walk into each room of my home and describe clearly what I wished that room to look like. Something wonderful happened! I described exactly how many pens and pencils I wanted, the kind of paper I wanted beside the telephone, and so forth. It became elaborate, energizing and thrilling.

Few people have taken the time to find out what really excites them, energizes them and motivates them.

Something interesting happened in my personal meditation time some weeks ago. I had been a little concerned that my interests frequently changed. For example, the colors my decorator would select for my home would be exciting and thrilling to me. I felt that I would never want to change my mind about them for years to come. A few weeks later, I discovered another combination of colors that excited me *again*. Obviously, I did not feel comfortable about suddenly changing everything that had been done in my home. Nor did I really have the finances to do so. I bought a car. I loved it...for about three weeks. *Then, I was bored and wanted a change.*

I felt impressed of The Holy Spirit to begin to write down a list of things that had never changed inside me over many years. It was quite a list of interesting things...and it really put my mind at ease that there was more stability within me than I realized. Many things have never changed whatsoever within me, such as my love for information, my desire to collect books and my excitement over receiving a rare new coin from a friend. Another thing that has never changed is my continual need to change my environment. Regardless of how beautifully my bedroom or kitchen were done...within twelve months or so, I was tired of it. That has been consistent.

Some things never change about you. What are they? Put down this book for about fifteen minutes.

Take a sheet of paper, and as quickly and thoroughly as possible, begin to document the things about yourself that have been pretty consistent over the years. Go ahead. Do it now.

Now, after you have done this, you will begin to get a fairly accurate and specific photograph of certain things that you want in your life and around you *daily*. You will also get an awareness of the *quality* of life you are struggling to experience.

Some years ago, I asked a consultant to come into my offices for several days. He was to discuss any complaints or ideas with each of my staff. Then I wanted him to compile a report, unbiased and unprejudiced, as to what he thought about our ministry organization. He *interrogated* me and *questioned* me for hours. He would take long walks with me and ride in the car; even while I was in crusades, we would talk on the phone. His *constant questioning* sharpened my focus remarkably. I have never forgotten it.

He was relentless in collecting data about my personal needs, desires and appetites towards life.

When were the *happiest* moments of my life?

What days did I seem to enjoy life *more* than usual?

What were the three biggest problems I thought about the most...*every day?*

Who were the people that were *stressful* for me to be around?

Who were the people in whose presence I was the most *relaxed?*

How did I want to be remembered?

What did I consider to be the *most important task* that I did each *day?* Each *week?* Each *month?*

If I had to eliminate fifty percent of my entire ministry workload, *what would I delete?*

If I were to have a sudden health crisis, experience a heart attack or some other medical emergency, what would I change *first* about my *daily lifestyle?*

Riveting questions were hurled at me continually. Slowly but surely, a remarkable understanding of what I *really* wanted out of life developed.

Here is a marvelous exercise. It could change your life forever. Ask one or two of your closest friends, who are skilled at analyzing and dissecting situations, to interrogate you—quizzing you relentlessly, extracting information from you until you have a perfect and complete photograph of the *invisible future* you are laboring to bring to reality. Something is driving you...pushing you toward your future. What is the *invisible dream* you are subconsciously trying to birth within you and your life?

Decisiveness Is Magnetic.

It is the catalyst for the aura that surrounds extraordinary and unforgettable people. They simply know *exactly* what they want.

When you are sitting in a restaurant sometime, do a little test. Carefully observe the entry of customers. Notice those who saunter and amble in as if they are not quite certain they have chosen the right restaurant. They slowly walk to their seats wondering if they should even stay at the restaurant, or should they select a different table.

Then, observe carefully those who stride in confidently and with a firm, clear and raised voice, express to the hostess of the restaurant, "Good evening! We need a table for four—by the window, if possible!" Notice how the hostess responds quickly, with enthusiasm and immediately begins to communicate to the other workers exactly what was requested.

When ordering your own meal at a restaurant, speak up. *Speak firmly. Do not mumble.*

Someone has said, "If you will raise your voice ten percent and walk twenty percent faster, you will generate remarkable new energy, compelling others to respond favorably to you and raising the level of self-confidence in every single person around you."

James said it this way, "But let him ask in faith, nothing wavering. For he that wavereth is like a wave of the sea driven with the wind and tossed. For let not that man think that he shall receive any thing of the Lord. A double minded man is unstable in all his ways," (James 1:6-8).

What happens when you are totally undecided about an issue or decision? There is a reason for it. It may be lack of *sufficient* information. It may be lack of *accurate* information. When this happens, simply declare with great decisiveness, "I have decided to wait 90 days until additional information arrives." You have retained the climate of *confidence* and *decisiveness.*

Make decisions with clarity.

Notice Ruth said it quite clearly, "Whither thou goest, I will go; and where thou lodgest, I will lodge," (Ruth 1:16).

She knew what she wanted. She *communicated* to Naomi what she wanted. She was *bold* about what she wanted.

Distinguish Between What Matters And What Does Not.

This is one of the secrets to becoming an Uncommon Achiever.

RECOMMENDED RESOURCES:
B-114   The Law of Recognition (247 pages/$10)
B-125   Seeds of Wisdom on Decision-Making (32 pages/$5
You Will Love Our Website...! www.TheWisdomCenter.tv

❧ 2 ❧

BE WILLING TO GO WHERE YOU HAVE NEVER GONE BEFORE

━━━━━➤⊙⥽━━━━━

Geography Makes A Difference.

"Also I heard the voice of the Lord, saying, Whom shall I send, and who will go for us? Then said I, Here am I; send me," (Isaiah 6:8).

Atmosphere matters. Pineapples do well in Hawaii. They do not do very well in Alaska. The *climate* is important for any Seed to grow.

You too, are a Seed. Your business and your product are like Seeds. It is true that you may need to change locations and situations to unlock the full potential of your success.

Success requires people. You will never succeed without networking with many different kinds of people. They may not be accessible. You may have to leave the comforts of your home to reach them to achieve extraordinary success.

Recently, I was amazed by what I saw in the life of Jesus. He was constantly in *movement,* constantly changing *locations.*

"When He was come down from the mountain, great multitudes followed Him," (Matthew 8:1). "And when Jesus was entered into Capernaum, there came unto Him a centurion, beseeching Him," (Matthew 8:5). "And when Jesus was come into Peter's house, He saw his wife's mother laid, and sick of a fever," (Matthew 8:14). "And when He was entered into a ship, His disciples followed Him," (Matthew 8:23). "And when He was come to the other side into the country of the Gergesenes, there met Him two possessed with devils, coming out of the tombs, exceeding fierce, so that no man might pass by that way," (Matthew 8:28).

Jesus was constantly arising, departing and going to new places. He sought to be around new people of varied backgrounds.

Some people will not come where you are. You have to go to their home, their town and their environment.

Jesus told His disciples to go to the Upper Room. They were to tarry there until they received the marvelous experience of The Holy Spirit. (See Luke 24:49.)

He gave this instruction to five hundred of His followers. Three hundred and eighty disobeyed Him. Even after they had observed His resurrection and His miracle life, only one hundred and twenty out of the five hundred actually followed His instruction. (See Acts 1:15.) But, those who were willing to go to a different *place*—the Upper Room, received the marvelous outpouring of The Holy Spirit.

Abraham, the patriarch of the Israelites, had to make *geographical changes* before his success was birthed. (See Genesis 12:1-2.)

Joseph found his incredible success in *another country*...Egypt. (See Genesis 41:39-44.)

Ruth *willingly left* her heathen family in Moab and went to Bethlehem with Naomi, where she met

Boaz, a financial giant of the community, and married him. (See Ruth 1:16-19, 4:13.)

It is normal to move toward those who are easily accessible.

Sometimes, you have to go *somewhere* you have never been before you taste the extraordinary success that you want to experience.

This is one of the secrets to becoming an Uncommon Achiever.

The Atmosphere
You Create Determines
The Product
You Produce.

-MIKE MURDOCK

CREATE THE ENVIRONMENT THAT KEEPS YOU STIMULATED

Atmosphere Matters.

The Atmosphere You Create Determines The Product You Produce.

Invest whatever is necessary to create the *atmosphere* that motivates you.

Your chosen focus requires a unique climate.

Your *surroundings* are so important. Your *atmosphere* must receive your attention. It will not happen automatically. You must control the atmosphere around your life or it will control you.

15 Keys In Creating The Climate And Atmosphere You Need

1. *Your Climate Influences The Decisions You Make.* When you are in a high end fashion clothing store, the music is often *quiet, classical* or *dignified.* When you go into a store where the younger generation makes purchases, the music is *fast, upbeat* and *energizing.* The merchants have created an environment that *influences* you to buy.

2. *Your Surroundings Contain Colors That Affect You Emotionally.* Many years ago, I read where a certain shade of pink was used in prisons to reduce violence and fights. Some say that bodybuilders can

lose one third of their ability if they look at a pink wall while working out. *Colors affect us.* Colors affect our strength, our enthusiasm and the decisions we make.

3. *Everyone Needs Something Different Around Them.* You must discern what environment and atmosphere brings out the best in you.

When I need energy and must move quickly from project to project, I love to listen to praise music that is energizing and exciting. When I want to ponder and reflect, I love to listen to slower, more worshipful music. I know the value of protecting the climate around myself.

4. *Nobody Else Can Create Your Atmosphere For You.* You must discern it and pursue it for yourself.

5. *Nobody Else Is Responsible For Providing You With The Climate You Desire.* It is your life, your needs and your decisions.

6. *You Will Not Do Your Very Best Until Everything Around You Is In Place.* Yes, you may achieve and be productive to a degree. But, you can multiply the results of your life when the things around you strengthen and motivate you.

7. *What You See Controls What You Desire.* When you see a billboard advertising hamburgers, you suddenly receive a desire for hamburgers. That is why you must put around yourself pictures and images of the things you want.

8. *What You Are Viewing Daily Affects What You Desire To Do.* When children see the playground at McDonald's, they are suddenly inspired to stop everything and go play.

9. *Keep Around You Photographs Of Things You*

Want In Your Future. It may be a boat you want to buy, a home you want to live in or a picture of yourself twenty pounds lighter. These images are influencing the direction your decision will take you.

10. *Your Environment Is Worth Any Investment In Music And Equipment*. Buy a stereo or whatever it takes to sculpture your ideal environment—get the best possible.

Every morning, I listen to the Scriptures on cassette tape. That is the first thing I do each day. Yes, they cost. The cassette recorder costs. My future and my emotions are *worth any investment*.

I purchase candles that smell the best, strongest and last the longest. Placing them around my room helps provide the most incredible atmosphere of reflection, warmth and caring. *I need that*. My heart *requires* it. If *I* do not do it, it will not be done. Because my life is so vital to me, I invest *whatever is necessary*.

A few days ago, I spent over $100 on several CDs. Yet, when I purchased them, I really was not just purchasing some music on compact discs. I was *purchasing an atmosphere*.

You see, this morning, after listening to the Bible on tape, I turned the CD player on. On the six CDs were birds, a sparkling, flowing fountain and peaceful music. Within seconds, I felt like I was under the trees, alone and quiet, *tasting* the richness of God's nature around me. Yet, I was in my bedroom! I did not have to spend $2,000 to take a vacation to Honolulu. I simply needed an investment in my atmosphere—the appropriate CDs.

11. *Your Investment In Interior Decorating Can*

Make A Huge Difference In Your Productivity. A new rug, a picture on the wall, a vase with a rose, every small thing can *increase* the warmth and caring of your environment.

12. *Invest The Effort And Experimentation To Discover What You Really Need Around You.* It is wonderful to explore variations of climates and environments. An interior decorator, the suggestions of a friend or your own personal visits to different stores can help you discover the atmosphere you prefer to work in, play around in or simply relax and rest in. Each atmosphere produces a *different* emotion.

13. *Do Not Wait On Others To Initiate Changes In Your Environment.* Make any investment necessary to create the kind of environment that inspires *you* toward excellence and the improvement of *your* life.

14. *Your Atmosphere Can Often Determine Your Productivity.* Many businesses have discovered an *increase* in unity and employee morale when they played music quietly throughout their offices.

15. *What You See Affects The Decisions You Are Making.* It does not cost you a fortune to create a favorable atmosphere. Just think... look around and ask questions. *Explore a little. Experiment.*

Invest whatever is necessary to create the atmosphere you want to surround you.

This is one of the secrets to becoming an Uncommon Achiever.

4

TREASURE AND PROTECT YOUR FLOW OF PASSION

Passion Is Power.

You Will Only Have Significant Success With Something That Is An Obsession. An obsession is when something *consumes* your thoughts and time.

You Will Only Be Remembered In Life For Your Obsession. Henry Ford is remembered for the automobile. Thomas Edison...inventions. Billy Graham...evangelism. Oral Roberts...healing. The Wright Brothers...the airplane.

Passion is desire.

It includes the desire to change, serve or achieve a goal.

Men who succeed greatly possess great *passion.* They are *consumed* and *obsessed.* It burns within them like fire. Nothing else matters to them but the completion of the instructions of God in their lives.

Isaiah was passionate. "For the Lord God will help me; therefore shall I not be confounded: therefore have I set my face like a flint, and I know that I shall not be ashamed," (Isaiah 50:7).

The Apostle Paul was passionate. "Brethren, I count not myself to have apprehended: but this one thing I do, forgetting those things which are behind, and reaching forth unto those things which are before,

I press toward the mark for the prize of the high calling of God in Christ Jesus," (Philippians 3:13-14).

Jesus had a passion for His mission and goal in life. "For the Son of man is come to seek and to save that which was lost," (Luke 19:10). "How God anointed Jesus of Nazareth with the Holy Ghost and with power: Who went about doing good, and healing all that were oppressed of the devil; for God was with Him," (Acts 10:38).

Jesus *focused* on doing the exact instructions of His Heavenly Father (see John 5:19). He healed the sick. He noticed the lonely. He came to make people successful, to restore and repair their life to full fellowship with His Father.

His obsession took Him to the cross (see Hebrews 12:2). It took Him to the crucifixion. Eight inches of thorns were crushed into His brow. A spear punctured His side. Spikes were driven into His hands. Thirty-nine stripes of a whip tore His back to shreds. Four hundred soldiers spit upon His body. His beard was ripped from His face. He was *obsessed* with the salvation of mankind...*and He succeeded.*

You are instructed to develop a passion for the Word of God. The Lord spoke to Joshua about the Law and instructed him to "Turn not from it to the right hand or to the left, that thou mayest prosper whithersoever thou goest. This book of the law shall not depart out of thy mouth; but thou shalt meditate therein day and night, that thou mayest observe to do according to all that is written therein: for then thou shalt make thy way prosperous, and then thou shalt have good success," (Joshua 1:7-8).

Move toward His presence today. Habitually

schedule time in The Secret Place. "He that dwelleth in the secret place of the most High shall abide under the shadow of the Almighty," (Psalm 91:1). *In His presence, your passion for Him will grow from a tiny acorn to a huge oak within you.*

Wrong relationships will weaken your passion for your Assignment. Recently, I went to dinner with several friends after a service. Within one hour, the discussion had become filled with problems of people, with financial difficulties and with complaining attitudes. I was shocked at what had begun to grow within me. Though I had left the service with great joy, something began to die within me. As others discussed the difficult situations in their lives, or how difficult it was to reach their goals, I felt my own fire begin to go out.

Paul warned of such associations. "Be not deceived: evil communications corrupt good manners," (1 Corinthians 15:33).

Protect the Gift of Passion within you. Guard your focus every hour. Be ruthless with distractions. *Feed* the picture of your goals continually. *Watch* for the Four Enemies of Passion: fatigue, busyness, over-scheduling and putting God last on your daily schedule.

You may start small. You may start with very little. If what you love begins to consume your mind, your thoughts, your conversation, your schedule...*look* for extraordinary success.

Do you dread going to work every morning? Do you anxiously look at the clock toward closing time each afternoon? Is your mind wandering throughout the day towards other places or things you would love to be doing? Then you will probably not have much success at what you are doing.

Find something that *consumes* you...something that is worthy of building your entire life around. *Consider it.*

Uncommon Success will require Uncommon Passion.

Treasure and protect your flow of passion.

This is one of the secrets to becoming an Uncommon Achiever.

RECOMMENDED RESOURCES:

B-13   Seeds of Wisdom on Dreams & Goals (32 pages/$3)

B-74   The Assignment: The Dream & The Destiny, Vol. 1 (164 pages/$10)

B-76   The Mentor's Manna on Assignment (32 pages/$3)

B-101   The 3 Most Important Things in Your Life (240 pages/$10)

TS-14   How to Stay Motivated to Achieve Your Dream (6 tapes/$30)

WCPL-18   Learning the Art of Celebration (CD/$10)

WCPL-30   Dealing with the Heartache of Disappointment (CD/$10)

CONSTANTLY CONSULT THE COUNSEL OF OTHERS IN YOUR DECISION-MAKING

Learn To Reach.

The Proof Of Humility Is The Willingness To Reach.

"Where no counsel is, the people fall: but in the multitude of counsellors there is safety," (Proverbs 11:14).

A famous billionaire of our day was trained by his father. In one of his recent books he said that he *called* his father a dozen times a week. He also telephones his own office twelve times a day. He said, "If I do not constantly stay in touch with my business, it is gone."

Stay in touch with your supervisor, your boss...anyone who supervises you, mentors you or is *guiding you into something you want to accomplish. Stay in touch regularly.*

Jesus was brilliant. He was a miracle worker. He *constantly consulted* His Heavenly Father. "Then answered Jesus and said unto them, Verily, verily, I say unto you, The Son can do nothing of himself, but what he seeth the Father do: for what things soever he doeth, these also doeth the Son likewise," (John 5:19).

Jesus was open to His Father about His feelings. In the garden of Gethsemane, He cried, "O my Father, if it be possible, let this cup pass from me: nevertheless not as I will, but as Thou wilt," (Matthew 26:39).

Jesus was persistent in pursuing His Father. "He went away again the second time, and prayed," (Matthew 26:42). Jesus felt alone. He lived in our world. He felt feelings you feel. He is our elder brother and, *He was not too proud to reach.*

Know the power of connection. *Create contact.* Know, this is the first step toward increase. *Somebody is a link to your future success.* Tomorrow hinges on your ability to pursue them. *Do it!*

This is one of the secrets to becoming an Uncommon Achiever.

Our Prayer Together...

"Father, give me the intelligence and humility to consult those who are guiding me. Put in me the desire to remain humble and seek after You every day. Father, please keep me from becoming too proud to reach. In Jesus' name. Amen."

RECOMMENDED RESOURCES:

TS-37   31 Secrets of The Uncommon Mentor (6 tapes/$30)

~ 6 ~

NEVER MAKE AN IMPORTANT DECISION WHEN YOU ARE TIRED

Tired Eyes Rarely See A Great Future.

When I am weary, I am not the same person. I do not have the same kind of faith, the same kind of enthusiasm and the same kind of patience as I do when I am rested, strengthened and feeling good in my spirit.

When You Are Tired...

1. *Mountains Look Bigger.* I do not understand it, but it is true. When I am tired at night, things that normally would appear *simple,* suddenly feel very *burdensome* and *complex* to me. Tasks that usually require a minimal effort, suddenly seem too much to take on.

2. *Valleys Seem Deeper.* Discouraging factors seem to *enlarge.* Disappointments seem keener and *stronger* when my body is worn out.

3. *Offenses Come Easier.* I seem more easily offended than I normally would be. *Little things become big.*

When I am tired, I begin to replay over in my mind, wrongs that people have done to me.

When I am rested, my mind moves to positive, wonderful and glorious dreams...things I want to accomplish and do.

Fatigue affects me in the opposite manner.

Jesus understood this. That is why He encouraged His disciples to "Come ye yourselves apart into a desert place, and rest a while," (Mark 6:31). One of our great presidents once said that he would never make a decision past 3:00 in the afternoon. He was too tired and weary to consider every option available.

4. *You Become Less Tolerant Of The Views And Needs Of Others*. When others are weary, they seem less understanding of your own opinions and views, also.

5. *Your Focus Is More On What You Want Instead Of The Appropriate Method For Achieving It.*

6. *Your Focus Turns To Short-Term Goals Rather Than Long-Term Goals.*

7. *Your Words Become Rash, Hasty And Usually Inappropriate.*

8. *You Become Unwilling To Invest Appropriate And Sufficient Time For Planning Ahead On A Project.*

9. *You Begin To Meditate On Your Own Mistakes And The Mistakes Of Others.* There is a Scripture that indicates that satan wants to wear out the saints. I believe it. "And he shall speak great words against the most High, and shall wear out the saints of the most High, and think to change times and laws: and they shall be given into his hand until a time and times and the dividing of time," (Daniel 7:25).

Rest Will Restore.

Never make important decisions unless you are strengthened, mentally alert and spiritually perceptive.

This is one of the secrets to becoming an Uncommon Achiever.

≈ 7 ≈

DO NOT BE AFRAID TO FAIL EN ROUTE TO YOUR SUCCESS

"No" Simply Means "Ask Again."
All Men Fall; The Great Ones Get Back Up.

Stay persistent. "And let us not be weary in well doing: for in due season we shall reap, if we faint not," (Galatians 6:9).

Stop for a moment. *Review* your past experiences. You encountered rejection when you were a child. Some of your schoolmates may not have liked you. But you made it any way, did you not?

Rejection is not fatal. It is merely someone's opinion.

Jesus experienced more rejection than any human who ever lived on earth. He was born in a stable. He was born as an *outcast* in society. (Even today, television talk show hosts *belittle* and make fun of Him and those who follow Him. The name of Jesus is used daily as a curse word by millions.) His own people *rejected* Him. "He came unto His own, and His own received Him not," (John 1:11).

Did He quit? When Judas betrayed Him, did He allow Himself to become demoralized? *No.*

Jesus knew that He did not have to close every sale to be a success. He went on to the others, who discerned His value. "But as many as received Him, to them gave He power to become the sons of God, even to them that believe on His name," (John 1:12).

He knew His *worth*. He knew His *product*.

Jesus knew His critics would die...but His plan was *eternal*.

He was willing to experience a season of pain...to create an eternity of gain (see Hebrews 12:2). Some things last longer than rejection...your goals and dreams.

Move beyond your scars. Not everyone will celebrate you. Not everyone will welcome your future.

Someone needs what you have. Your contribution is an absolute necessity for their success. *Discern it.*

Pharisees rejected Jesus. The religious sect, called Sadducees, rejected Him. Religious leaders despised Christ. Those who should have recognized His worth, wanted to destroy Him (see Matthew 26:3-4).

Jesus risked rejection to become the golden link between man and God (see Hebrews 12:2).

Babe Ruth was famous for many years as the home-run king in baseball history. Many people have never realized that he also had more strikeouts than any other batter! They have not remembered his losses. They merely remember his *successes*. He was willing to risk a strikeout to hit that home run.

Most great salesmen say that knowing that fourteen out of fifteen people will say no, merely inspires them to hurry and make their presentations to as many as possible, to reach that one who will accept.

Jesus taught His disciples how to handle rejection. "And whosoever shall not receive you, nor hear your words, when ye depart out of that house or city, shake off the dust of your feet," (Matthew 10:14).

So, climb off your recliner. Make that telephone call. Write that letter.

Sooner or later you will succeed.

Do not be afraid to fail en route to your success.

This is one of the secrets to becoming an Uncommon Achiever.

Obedience Turns
A Common Instruction
Into An Uncommon Miracle.

-MIKE MURDOCK

☙ 8 ☙

BE WILLING TO START SMALL

Little Things Matter.

Small hinges swing huge doors. Small keys unlock vaults containing millions of dollars. A little steering determines the direction of a huge semi-truck.

One small finger dialing the telephone can start a business transaction of one billion dollars. *Never despise small beginnings.* "For who hath despised the day of small things?" (Zechariah 4:10).

Many will never become an Uncommon Achiever because they want their beginning to be spectacular.

I am reminded of the fascinating story of Naaman, the captain of the host of the king of Syria. He was a leper. When he went to the house of Elisha, the prophet sent him a simple instruction. Elisha sent a message to him to go and wash in the Jordan River seven times.

Naaman was infuriated. He had a different mental picture of how his healing would occur. One of his servants made an interesting statement, "My father, if the prophet had bid thee do some great thing, wouldest thou not have done it? how much rather then, when he saith to thee, Wash, and be clean?" (2 Kings 5:13).

The Assignment from Elisha was simple, clear and direct. Naaman was to go wash in Jordan seven times.

When you do the simple, the supernatural occurs.

Small beginnings often have great endings.

Jesus understood this principle. He was born in a stable, in a small town of Bethlehem. His beginning did not matter to Him...*He knew His destiny.* He was aware of the greatness of His destination. One of His greatest statements ever is "He that is faithful in that which is least is faithful also in much: and he that is unjust in the least is unjust also in much," (Luke 16:10).

Attention To Details Produces Excellence. It is the difference between extraordinary champions and losers. Do not despise and feel insignificant in your small acts of obedience while giving birth to your Assignment.

One of the great evangelists of our day began his ministry duplicating tapes for his mentor. Hour after hour, day after day, he sat and duplicated tapes. He listened to each tape over and over. He *served.* He *ministered.* He *assisted.* It was *the beginning* of a significant ministry.

Ruth began life as an ignorant Moabite heathen girl. Her attention to the small details of her Assignment, (Naomi), positioned her as the great-grandmother of David and ushered in the lineage of Jesus. (See Ruth 4:13, 21-22.)

Abigail brought lunch to the starving man, David. She became his wife (see 1 Samuel 25:10-42).

When Jesus wanted to produce a great miracle, He always gave a *small* instruction.

Little things mattered to Him. Little things *still* matter to Him. Notice the small, seemingly insignificant instructions that Jesus gave. They almost seemed ridiculous. Some might think these were instructions given to children, but none of them were. Rather, they were given to grown men...to mature adults.

▶ "And said unto him, Go, wash in the pool of Siloam, (which is by interpretation, Sent.) He went his way therefore, and washed, and came seeing," (John 9:7). This was a big miracle. Yes, a blind man was healed from a lifetime of blindness.

▶ "Now when he had left speaking, he said unto Simon, Launch out into the deep, and let down your nets for a draught," (Luke 5:4). This small instruction produced the greatest catch of fish the disciples had ever gathered.

▶ "Jesus saith unto them, Fill the waterpots with water. And they filled them up to the brim," (John 2:7). It produced the greatest wine anyone had ever tasted...ever. It happened at the marriage of Canaan.

▶ "I say unto thee, Arise, and take up thy bed, and go thy way into thine house," (Mark 2:11). What was the result? A man sick of the palsy, *immediately arose,* took up his bed, and went forth before them all and many glorified God because of it.

▶ "He said, Bring them hither to me," (Matthew 14:18). These words were spoken regarding the five loaves and two fishes, the lunch of a lad. What happened afterwards has been preached around the world. Thousands were fed miraculously, and at the conclusion, each of the twelve disciples had a basketful to bring home!

▶ Great miracles do not require *great* instructions.

▶ Great miracles require *obeyed* instructions.

A student in Bible school sits in chapel daily awaiting a neon sign in the Heavens declaring, "Bob, go to Calcutta, India." It never happens. Why? Bob has not obeyed the first instruction. "Bob, go to the prayer room at 7:00 a.m."

Obedience Turns A Common Instruction Into An Uncommon Miracle.

God does not give great instructions to great men.

God gives Uncommon Instructions to *common* men. When you obey that instruction, greatness is birthed. "If ye be willing and obedient, ye shall eat the good of the land," (Isaiah 1:19).

Nothing you will do today is small in the eyes of God.

You may have small beginnings.

Be Willing To Start Small.

This is one of the secrets to becoming an Uncommon Achiever.

RECOMMENDED RESOURCES:

B-20   Seeds of Wisdom on Obedience (32 pages/$3)

B-183   31 Scriptures Every Achiever Should Memorize (32 pages/$3)

TS-08   The Strategy of Hourly Obedience (6 tapes/$30)

You Will Love Our Website: www.TheWisdomCenter.tv

❧ 9 ❧

FOCUS YOUR ENERGY ON YOUR FUTURE

━━━━►❯◦❮━━━━

Become A "Tomorrow Thinker."
Make Your Future So Big Yesterday Disappears.
Ruth created a future far different from her past.

Ruth was a Moabitess girl raised in heathenism. Moab was the son of incest between Lot and his daughter.

Ruth married Boaz who, according to one writer, had come through the loins of a temple prostitute by the name of Rahab. God put them together...and ushered in the lineage of Jesus Christ (see Ruth 4:13-22).

Ruth and Boaz produced Obed. Obed produced Jesse. Jesse produced David. David ushered in the lineage of Jesus Christ. Who was Ruth?

Ruth was the great-grandmother of David, the greatest warrior Israel has ever known. She was the great-great-grandmother of one of the wisest men who ever lived on earth, Solomon. Through her and Boaz came the precious Son of the living God, Jesus of Nazareth.

God Never Consults Your Past To Decide Your Future. Satan may remind you of yesterday's mistakes. Do not listen to him. God never reads your diary. Your past is over. Act like it. Talk like it. Live like it.

Your best days are *ahead* of you.

Your worst days are *behind* you.

There Are 3 Kinds Of People You Permit In Your Life

There are Yesterday, Today and Tomorrow people.

Those that God used yesterday may not have a place in your future. Do not worry about it. Move quickly toward the promises of God. Prepare to enter your future without yesterday people.

You will not make the mistakes of yesterday again. You have more knowledge today than you have ever had in your whole lifetime.

You have learned from the *pain.*

You have learned from your *losses.*

You have watched carefully and documented what has happened in other people's lives. Do not fear that yesterday will crawl behind you like a predator and choke you to death.

It will not happen. "Remember ye not the former things, neither consider the things of old. Behold, I will do a new thing; now it shall spring forth; shall ye not know it? I will even make a way in the wilderness, and rivers in the desert," (Isaiah 43:18-19).

"Forgetting those things which are behind, and reaching forth unto those things which are before, I press toward the mark for the prize of the high calling of God in Christ Jesus," (Philippians 3:13-14).

The Holy Spirit is your Enabler. "But ye shall receive power, after that the Holy Ghost is come upon you," (Acts 1:8).

The Holy Spirit is your Comforter. "But when the

Comforter is come, whom I will send unto you from the Father, even the Spirit of truth, which proceedeth from the Father, he shall testify of Me," (John 15:26).

The Holy Spirit is your Teacher. "He shall teach you all things, and bring all things to your remembrance, whatsoever I have said unto you," (John 14:26).

The Holy Spirit is the Revealer of those things which are to come. "Howbeit when He, the Spirit of truth, is come, He will guide you into all truth," (John 16:13).

It fascinates me that Ruth was willing to leave everything comfortable to pursue her future. Her kinfolks were in her past. She refused to let her upbringing and her religious background become the noose around her neck that sabotaged her future. She refused to let her past rob her of the potential of tomorrow. (See Ruth 1:16-18.)

I have said many times that *Intolerance Of Your Present Schedules Your Future.* As long as you can adapt to the present...you really do not have a future.

Ruth refused to build her future around her past. Some of us remember painful experiences from yesterday. We have built our entire lifestyle around that experience. Our conversations are consumed with occurrences of ten years ago.

This is dangerous.

It is devastating.

When you discuss your past, you perpetuate it. Words impart life. When you continually replay painful confrontations and situations of the past, you are giving life to them...you are giving a future to them. *When You Replay The Past, You Poison The*

Present.

Achievers permit yesterday to die.

Ruth did. She did not try to straddle the fence. She refused to become the link between the past and her future.

She totally *abandoned* the empty relationships of her past.

One of the saddest pictures is found in the life of the great patriarch, Abraham. He insisted on bringing Lot, his nephew, with him into the future God had prepared. *Lot was a distraction.* Most of Abraham's continual problems could be traced to the presence of Lot. You see, God had told Abraham to leave his kinfolks and move on to a different territory. He insisted on bringing someone he was comfortable with—to the detriment of his future.

Yesterday people will rarely enjoy your future.

It is natural and normal to want to bring everyone close to us into the chapters of our future success. Few will qualify.

Your future must be earned.

It is not guaranteed. It is not the same for everyone. Your future is a Harvest produced by the Seeds you are willing to sow. Bringing yesterday people into the future is like using old wineskins for the new wine of tomorrow. It simply will not work.

So, prepare to enter your future without yesterday people. God will bring the right associations *with* you. He has scheduled outstanding divine connections beyond your greatest and wildest dreams.

Move away from yesterday. You have exhausted its benefits. Refuse to waste your energy on repairing it. Rather, rebuild by focusing on your future.

Certainly, yesterday can be a reservoir of Wisdom and information. You are not forfeiting loyalty. You are not forgetting the precious lives God used mightily for your continued survival and success. However, you are refusing to abort your future joys and victories by replaying the memories of yesterday's painful experiences.

Paul refused to wallow in the tears of his past. Few made greater mistakes than he. He caused people to be cast into prison. Christians were murdered...*because of him.* He held the coats of those who stoned the great deacon, Stephen. Yet, he refused to forfeit his future by focusing on his past.

His mistakes were *over.*

His sins were *behind* him.

His name had been *changed.*

Eventually, you will be forced to make a major decision in your life. Make the decision to totally abandon your memories, and empty your energy into the palace of your future.

Your conversation must become more creative.

Start using your imagination instead of your memories. Meet new friends. Experience new places.

Ruth knew when she had exhausted the benefits of her present season. This truth is so powerful and important.

Every season in your life contains certain advantages. Whether it is one month of a relationship or 90 days on a job, you must discern the divine purposes of God in every situation in your life. You must discern the divine purpose of God in *every relationship.*

Never linger in a conversation with someone when

it is over. Would you keep chewing the same mouthful of food for three hours? *Of course not.*

Would you keep reading the same page of a book for three days? *Of course not.* Would you leave a broken record on at the same groove replaying the same note over and over again for several hours? *Of course not.* Would you keep brushing your teeth for twelve hours in a row? *Of course not.*

When something is finished...*it is finished.*

Discern it. Recognize it. Look for it. Consistently be intuitive and discerning when a specific season in your life has concluded. Then, move quickly and expectantly to the next season God has arranged for you.

This quality made Ruth *unforgettable.*

This quality makes Achievers *unforgettable.*

Focus your energy on your future.

This is one of the secrets to becoming an Uncommon Achiever.

RECOMMENDED RESOURCES:
B-11   Dream Seeds (106 pages/$9)
B-13   Seeds of Wisdom on Dreams & Goals
            (32 pages/$3)
B-103   Secrets of The Journey, Vol. 7 (32 pages/$5)

≈ **10** ≈

SET GOALS AND UPDATE THEM CONTINUOUSLY

Decide What You Really Want.

You Will Never Leave Where You Are Till You Decide Where You Would Rather Be.

In 1952, a prominent university discovered that only *three* out of one-hundred graduates had written down a clear list of goals. Ten years later, their follow-up study showed that *three* percent of the graduating class had accomplished more financially than the remaining ninety-seven percent of the class.

Those *three* percent were the *same graduates* who had *written down their goals.* "Write the vision, and make it plain upon tables, that he may run that readeth it," (Habakkuk 2:2).

When you decide exactly *"what"* you want, the *"how to do it"* will emerge.

When Your Heart Decides The Destination, Your Mind Will Design The Map To Reach It.

Jesus knew His purpose and mission. "For the Son of man is come to seek and to save that which was lost," (Luke 19:10).

Jesus knew the product He had to offer. "The thief cometh not, but for to steal, and to kill, and to destroy: I am come that they might have life, and that they might have it more abundantly," (John 10:10).

Jesus had a sense of destiny. He knew where He wanted to go. He knew where people needed Him. (Read John 4:3.)

Jesus knew that Achievers were detail oriented. "For which of you, intending to build a tower, sitteth not down first, and counteth the cost, whether he have sufficient to finish it?" (Luke 14:28).

Take four sheets of paper. At the top of sheet number one, write,

"My Lifetime Dreams and Goals."

Now write in total detail everything you would like to become, do or have during your lifetime. *Dream in detail on paper.*

Now, take sheet number two and write,

"My Twelve-Month Goals."

Now list everything you want to get done within the next twelve months.

Now, take the third sheet of paper and write,

"My Thirty-Day Goals."

Now write out in detail what you would like to accomplish for the next thirty days.

Now, take a fourth sheet of paper and write,

"My Ideal Success Daily Routine."

Now write down the six most important rituals you can do daily...

The Secret Of Your Future Is Hidden In Your Daily Routine.

Set your goals...realizing that *your goals will change throughout your life.*

Someday, you will look back at this very moment and be amazed at the goals you presently have. Things so vital to you at twenty years of age will become unimportant to you at thirty.

When I was beginning my ministry, I wanted very much to minister in many different states and cities.

Times have changed. Today, staying home excites me. Knowing that my books are being read in many places is far more satisfying to me than traveling. *The greatest goal of my life today is staying in my Secret Place of prayer and writing what The Holy Spirit teaches me through His Word and daily experiences.*

These kinds of good changes will happen to you too.

6 Helpful Tips Concerning Your Dreams And Goals

1. *Invest One Hour In Writing Down Clearly The Goals That Really Matter To You At This Point.* Keep it *confidential* and *private,* "Write the vision, and make it plain upon tables, that he may run that readeth it," (Habakkuk 2:2).

2. *Permit Unexciting Dreams Of Yesterday To Die.* Stop pursuing something that does not have the ability to excite you anymore. Do not feel obligated to keep trying to obtain expired goals...if you are in a different place in your life. (See Isaiah 43:18-19.)

3. *Do Not Depend On Others To Understand Your Dreams And Goals.* Permit them their *individuality,* also. They have every right to love the things they love. Refuse however, to be intimidated by their efforts to persuade you to move in a different direction with *your* life.

4. *Never Make Permanent Decisions Because Of Temporary Feelings.* One young lady got so excited about a new friend that she dropped the lease on her own apartment and moved into the apartment of her

friend. Within a week, she realized her mistake!

5. *Avoid Intimate Relationships With Those Who Do Not Really Respect Your Dreams.* You will have to sever ties. *Wrong people do not always leave your life voluntarily.* Life is too short to permit discouragers close to you. "And have no fellowship with the unfruitful works of darkness, but rather reprove them," (Ephesians 5:11).

6. *Anticipate Changes In Your Goals.* Your present feelings and opinions are not permanent. *New* experiences are coming. *New* relationships are ahead. Stay conscious of this.

When you assess and evaluate your goals, you will unclutter your life of the unnecessary.

Set goals and update them continuously.

This is one of the secrets to becoming an Uncommon Achiever.

⁓ 11 ⁓

INVEST TIME IN YOUR PLAN

Champions Plan.

Champions Make Decisions That Create The Future They Desire; Losers Make Decisions That Create The Present They Desire.

"Through wisdom is an house builded; and by understanding it is established: And by knowledge shall the chambers be filled with all precious and pleasant riches," (Proverbs 24:3-4).

What is a plan? A plan is a written list of arranged actions necessary to achieve your desired goal. "Write the vision, and make it plain upon tables, that he may run that readeth it," (Habakkuk 2:2).

Jesus planned your future. "In My Father's house are many mansions: if it were not so, I would have told you. I go to prepare a place for you," (John 14:2).

Think for a moment. God *scheduled* the birth, the crucifixion and resurrection of His Son before the foundation of the earth. "And all that dwell upon the earth shall worship him, whose names are not written in the book of life of the Lamb slain from the foundation of the world," (Revelation 13:8).

I think it is quite fascinating that God would schedule a meal, the marriage supper, six thousand years ahead of time! "Blessed are they which are called unto the marriage supper of the Lamb," (Revelation 19:9).

God always honored men who planned.

Noah *planned* the building of the ark.

Solomon, the wisest man who ever lived on earth, *took time to plan* the building of the temple.

Moses, the great deliverer, who brought the Israelites out of Egypt, took time to *plan* the tabernacle.

Your Bible is the plan of God for you, the world and eternity. It is the undeniable proof that God thinks ahead. Most of the Bible is *prophecy,* a description of the future before it ever occurs.

Jesus taught, "For which of you, intending to build a tower, *sitteth not down first, and counteth the cost,* whether he have sufficient to finish it? Lest haply, after he hath laid the foundation, and is not able to finish it, all that behold it begin to mock him, Saying, This man began to build, and was not able to finish. Or what king, going to make war against another king, sitteth not down first, and consulteth whether he be able with ten thousand to meet him that cometh against him with twenty thousand?" (Luke 14:28-31).

Make a list of things to do every day. Write six things you want to accomplish that day. Focus your total attention on each task. Assign each task to a *specific time. (If you cannot plan events for twenty-four hours in your life, what makes you think you will accomplish your desires for the next twenty-four years?)*

Think of each hour as an employee. *Delegate a specific Assignment to each hour.* What do you want to accomplish between 7 a.m. and 8 a.m.? Who should you telephone today?

Write out your plan clearly on a sheet of paper. *Successes are usually scheduled events.* Failures are not.

Planning is *laborious.* It is *tedious.* It is *meticulous.* It is *grilling, demanding* and *exhausting.* In my personal opinion, detailed planning is really never fun.

Champions Are Willing To Do Things They Hate To Create Something Else They Love.

Why do people avoid planning? Some avoid it because it is time consuming. They are so busy "mopping up the water" that they do not take the time to turn off the faucet!

The Secret Of Your Future Is Hidden In Your Daily Routine. Even ants think ahead. "Go to the ant, thou sluggard; consider her ways, and be wise: Which having no guide, overseer, or ruler, Provideth her meat in the summer, and gathereth her food in the harvest," (Proverbs 6:6-8).

Invest time in your plan.

This is one of the secrets to becoming an Uncommon Achiever.

RECOMMENDED RESOURCES:
B-137   Seeds of Wisdom on Productivity (32 pages/$5)
TS-45   The School of Wisdom #5/The Law of Order
          (6 tapes/$30)
WCPL-105 What Are Are You Doing With Your Cotton-Pickin
          Life? (CD/$10)

Success Is
The Fragrance Of Joy
When A Goal
Has Been Achieved.

-MIKE MURDOCK

❧ 12 ❧

FINISH WHAT YOU START

Uncommon Achievers Are Finishers.

Finishing births inner pleasure. "The desire accomplished is sweet to the soul," (Proverbs 13:19).

It is fun to be creative. It is exciting to always be giving birth to new ideas, thinking of new places to go or launching a new product. But, real champions... *complete things.* They are *follow-through* people.

Jesus was thirty years old when He started His ministry. His ministry went for three and a half years. He did many miracles. He touched many lives. He electrified the world through twelve men.

Hidden in the thousands of Scriptures is The Golden Principle that revealed His power. It happened on the horrible day of His crucifixion. He was taunted by thousands. A spear pierced His side. Spikes were driven into His hands. Eight inches of thorns were crushed into His brow. Blood had dried on His hair. Four hundred soldiers left spittle running down his body.

That is when He uttered perhaps the greatest sentence ever uttered on earth: "It is finished," (John 19:30). The sin of man could be forgiven. He paid the price. *The Plan was complete.*

He was the Lamb led to the slaughter (Acts 8:32).

He was the Chief Cornerstone (Ephesians 2:20).

The Prince of Peace had come (Isaiah 9:6).

Our great High Priest, the Son of God, was our Golden Link to the God of Heaven (Hebrews 4:14).

Jesus was a finisher. He finished what He started. The bridge that linked man to God was *complete.* Man could approach God without fear.

The Apostle Paul was a finisher (2 Timothy 4:7).

Solomon, the wisest man that ever lived was a finisher (1 Kings 6:14).

One famous multi-millionaire said, "I will pay a great salary to anyone who can complete an instruction that I give him."

Start completing *little things.* Write that "Thank You" note to your friend. Make those two telephone calls.

Obtain the spirit of a finisher. "And ye shall be hated of all men for My name's sake: but he that endureth to the end shall be saved," (Matthew 10:22).

This is one of the secrets of becoming an Uncommon Achiever.

RECOMMENDED RESOURCES:
WCPL-13 Master Secrets for Becoming an Uncommon Finisher (CD/$10)

⇜ **13** ⇝

MAKE NECESSARY ADJUSTMENTS CONTINUALLY

Appearance Matters.

People See What You Are Before They Hear What You Are.

Ruth worked in the fields gathering barley, or wheat, depending on the season. One day, she came home and was sitting there with Naomi. Her hair was probably matted...sweat pouring down her body. She was exhausted and worn out. Undoubtedly, she looked as bad as anyone could look at the end of a long, hard day.

Naomi gave her advice about approaching Boaz. "Wash thyself therefore, and anoint thee, and put thy raiment upon thee, and get thee down to the floor: but make not thyself known unto the man, until he shall have done eating and drinking," (Ruth 3:3).

Men respond to *sight.*

Women respond to *touch.*

Men and women are totally different creatures.

Needs *differ.*

Tastes *differ.*

Hygiene *matters.*

Appearance *matters.*

Ruth packaged herself for where she was going, instead of where she had been.

The attire of a *harlot* is discussed in the seventh chapter of Proverbs.

The attire of a *virtuous woman* is discussed in the thirty-first chapter of Proverbs.

In Genesis, Joseph shaved his beard and changed his raiment because he knew that the Egyptians hated beards. He wanted to *create a climate of acceptance* in the palace of Pharaoh (Genesis 41:14).

Even Timothy was instructed by the Apostle Paul on the appearance and clothing of women in the church. I attended an amazing seminar some months ago on appearance and how to create a sense of balance with clothing and the colors you wear.

Presentation Decides Desire.

Naomi was brilliant. She taught Ruth how to create for Boaz a memorable picture...*one that gave him a desire to reach.*

Some months ago, I was driving by a home. The wife was waving good-bye to her husband as he was backing out of the driveway. Her hair was in curlers. Her bathrobe looked torn, wrinkled and probably had a button or two missing. I was not close enough to smell her breath, but I certainly could imagine it! She was waving to him good-bye and giving him a permanent photograph of what was awaiting upon his return home. (Maybe that explained why he couldn't wait to get to work!)

I had to laugh inside. I could just imagine his thoughts of "home" as he drove by the billboards of beautiful ladies and walked into his office with everyone packaged nicely and attractively.

What am I saying? You must make yourself desirable for the man you desire. *Personal appearance matters.*

The president of the largest employment agency in the world said that over ninety percent of the people who are hired were hired because of their personal appearance.

You are a walking message system. People see what you are *before they hear* what you are.

Imagine riding on an airplane and noticing that the pilot has catsup all over his shirt. Imagine his hair uncombed. Imagine dirt all over the bottom of his shoes. Now, try to imagine sitting in the seat and noticing torn seat covers on your seat. Several light bulbs are smashed. What is your next thought? "I wonder if anyone has checked the engine? I wonder if there is enough fuel in the tanks? I wonder if they have had the mechanics provide accurate maintenance?"

Packaging determines whether you reach or withdraw.

Look at the products you purchase at the store. *Everything* you are buying is based on...*appearance.*

Make any change necessary today that will make you more desirable for your spouse. It may be braces on your teeth, taking your clothes to the cleaners for pressing, or finding the lipstick with exactly the right color for you.

This kind of attitude made Ruth an unforgettable woman, and this kind of attitude will make you an unforgettable Champion.

Make necessary adjustments.

This is one of the secrets to becoming an Uncommon Achiever.

Order Is Simply
The Accurate
Arrangement Of Things.

-MIKE MURDOCK

❧ 14 ❧

TAKE A SMALL STEP TOWARD ORDER EVERY DAY

Order Is...Accurate Arrangement Of Things.
Order is placing an item where it belongs. Order is keeping your shirts, ties and shoes in the appropriate place in your closet.

Every tiny act of your life will increase order or disorder around you. The purpose of order is to increase productivity and create comfort. When you walk into a room of order, you want to *stay*. Things are "right." You feel clean, energized and happy. When you walk into a room of clutter and disorder, an unexplainable agitation begins. Perhaps you cannot even identify it or understand it. *You were created for order*...anything that slows you down emotionally or mentally will become a distraction.

When you increase order in your life, you will increase your productivity. Filing cabinets, trays on the desk, and special places for folders make it easier to get your job done on time.

Have you ever shuffled paper after paper in search of a bill? Of course! When you finally located the bill, you were agitated and angry. It affected your entire day.

Disorder influences your attitude more than you could ever imagine. *Everything you are doing is affecting order in your life.* Think for a moment. You get up from your breakfast table. Either you will leave your plate on the table, or you will take it to the sink. The decision you make will either increase the order or disorder around you. (Leaving it on the table increases your workload and creates disorder. Taking it to the sink *immediately* brings order.)

It happened to me last night. I took off my suit coat and laid it over the chair. I did not really feel like taking it over to the closet and hanging it up. However, realizing that I was going to have to hang it up sooner or later, I walked over to the closet and hung up my coat. I increased order around myself immediately.

> ▶ Every moment, you are increasing order or creating disorder around your life.
> ▶ Small tiny actions, can eventually produce desired results.

Every person around you is increasing order or disorder. Some people have an *attitude* of disorder. They are unhappy unless everything is in disarray and cluttered. Others refuse to work in such an environment. Their productivity *requires* organization.

Somebody has said that the arrangement of things in your garage reveals much about your mind. (Somebody asked me once, "Does this mean if I do not have a garage, that I really do not have a mind either?" I certainly hope that is not the case, but I am certain psychologists have come to some pretty accurate conclusions.)

Why Do We Permit Disorder?

1.   *Many Of Us Were Raised With Those Who Are Unorganized.* Large families, busy life-styles, or small cramped apartments can contribute to our attitude.

2.   *Some People Do Not Know How To Separate And Organize Various Items Around Them.* They need assistance.

3.   *Some People Have Unusual Sensitivity And Are Simply Gifted In Keeping Order Around Them.*

4.   *Creative People Are Often Disorganized People.*

5.   *Busy People Moving From Place To Place Are Often Disorganized.* Their mind is on where they are *going* instead of *where they are.*

Helpful Hints

1.   *Recognize The Long-Term Chaos And Losses That Disorder Will Create.* If this continues, your momentum will eventually be destroyed along with your productivity. Successes will diminish.

2.   *Take A Long, Hard And Serious Look At Your Personality And What You Can Do To Take Steps Toward Change.*

3.   *Ask Others Who Are Gifted In Organization To Assist You And Keep You On Course.* I read that Donald Trump said that he hired one woman whose entire job is to keep things in order around him.

4.   *Do Not Berate Yourself And Become Overly Critical Because Of Your Lack Of Knowledge, Giftings Or Ability To Keep Things In Order.*

5.   *Recognize Those Whom God Puts Close To*

You Who Can Correct Things Around You And Keep Things In Order.

Don't try to justify yourself. Relax.

Take a small tiny step today toward putting things around you in order. It is commendable that you are planning to take an entire week of your vacation to put everything in order in your house next summer. However, I suggest you begin *this very moment* taking some steps to put things in place here in the room.

Just twenty minutes makes a major difference. Little hinges swing big doors. *You can get anywhere you want to go if you are willing to take enough small steps.*

So, take an important step toward order every moment of your life.

This is one of the secrets to becoming an Uncommon Achiever.

RECOMMENDED RESOURCES:
TS-45   The School of Wisdom #5 / The Law of Order
            (6 tapes/$30)
WCPL-42 7 Wisdom Keys for Organizing Your Life (CD/$10)
WCPL-56 12 Ingredients of a Perfect Day, Vols. 1-2 (2 CDs/$15)

15

MAKE THE GIFT OF HABIT WORK FOR YOU

Great Men Simply Have Great Habits.

The Secret Of Your Future Is Hidden In Your Daily Routine.

"Then said Jesus to those Jews which believed on him, If ye continue in my word, then are ye my disciples indeed," (John 8:31).

A well-known billionaire said, "I arrive at my office at 7:00 a.m. It is habit."

A best-selling novelist who has sold over one-million books said, "I get up at the same time every morning. I start writing at 8:00 a.m. and I quit at 4:00 each afternoon. I do it every day. It is habit."

Habit is a *gift* from God. *It simply means anything you do twice becomes easier.* Habit is the Creator's key in helping you succeed.

Jesus stayed busy. He traveled. He prayed for the sick. He taught and ministered. He supervised His disciples. He spoke to large crowds.

However, he had an important custom and habit. "And he came to Nazareth, where he had been brought up: and, as his custom was, he went into the synagogue on the sabbath day, and stood up for to read," (Luke 4:16).

Daniel *prayed* three times a day (Daniel 6:10).

The psalmist *prayed* seven times daily (Psalm 119:164).

The disciples of Jesus *met* on the first day of each week (Acts 20:7).

Great men simply have great habits.

Make the gift of habit work for you.

This is one of the secrets to becoming an Uncommon Achiever.

RECOMMENDED RESOURCES:
B-18   Seeds of Wisdom on Habits (32 pages/$3)
WCPL-56 12 Ingredients of a Perfect Day, Vols. 1-2 (2 CDs/$15)

16

NEVER DO WHAT A MACHINE CAN DO

Proper Equipment Increases Your Productivity.
Never have someone do a job that a machine can do instead. This is a humorous explanation of the advantages of proper equipment.

10 Advantages Of Using Appropriate Technology

1. *Machines Do Not Require Coaxing, Just Repair.*

2. *Machines Do Not Get Discouraged When Their Mother-in-law Comes To Town.*

3. *Machines Are Never Disloyal, Discussing Your Secrets With Everyone Else.*

4. *Your Machines Will Not File Grievance Reports Against You When You Fail To Meet Their Expectations.*

5. *Machines Do Not Require Medical Insurance, Sick Leave Or Time Off.*

6. *Machines Can Be Replaced Quickly And Easily Without Breaking Your Heart.*

7. *Machines Do Not Request A Retirement Fund And Want To Be Paid For The Years Ahead When They Don't Perform.*

8. *Machines Never Come To Work Late And Want To Leave Early.*

9. *Machines Will Work Through Lunch, Requiring No "Break Time."*

10. *Machines Never Interrupt The Productivity Of Other Machines, Slowing Down The Entire Project.*

6 Qualities Of True Achievers:

1. *They Will Find The Most Effective Equipment Possible To Do Their Present Job.*

2. *They Will Telephone Other Businesses Or Companies To Locate Appropriate Or Needed Machines And Equipment.*

3. *They Will Attend Seminars And Workshops That Increase Their Efficiency Or Skills On Computers And Other Machines.*

4. *They Will Inform Their Boss What Is Needed To Do The Job More Efficiently, More Accurately And Quickly.* He will usually do anything possible to make the hours of employees more effective and productive.

5. *They Will Continuously Evaluate Their Work.* What is slowing them down? What machine could make a big difference in the completion of their daily tasks and responsibilities?

6. *They Will Present Their Supervisors With Options, Costs And Potential Benefits Of Purchasing More Productive Machines.* Your staff will treasure them and learn to appreciate their own work load reduction because of technology. Machines decrease the opportunities for mistakes. They increase the staff's sense of progress and accomplishment. Search for appropriate equipment to accomplish your tasks

quickly.

Never do what a machine can do.

This is one of the secrets to becoming an Uncommon Achiever.

RECOMMENDED RESOURCES:

SOML-14 How to Develop Your Information System (CD/$10)

WCPL-55 How to Increase Your Effectiveness in Your Work-Place (3 CDs/$20)

WCPL-58 How to Customize Your Personal Time-Management System (CD/$10)

WCPL-92 Master Secrets in The Art of Asking, Vols. 1-4 (4 CDs/$25)

Money Does Not
Change You;
It Magnifies What
You Already Are.

-MIKE MURDOCK

17

NEVER EXPECT MONEY TO BE ENOUGH IN YOUR QUEST FOR FULFILLMENT

Rich People Are Not Always Happy People.
Money Does Not Change You; It Magnifies What You Already Are.

"Charge them that are rich in this world, that they be not highminded, nor trust in uncertain riches, but in the living God, who giveth us richly all things to enjoy," (1 Timothy 6:17).

Your hands can be *full* of money. Your head can be *full* of information. But if your heart is *empty,* your life is very *empty.*

Money is for movement...*not accumulation.* That is why the Bible talks about "the deceitfulness of riches."

Jesus saw this. He talked to the rich. He looked into their eyes and saw a longing for something that money could not buy. They came to Him late at night, when the crowds were gone. They were lonely. "For a man's life consisteth not in the abundance of the things which he possesseth," (Luke 12:15).

Solomon was a wealthy king. Yet he confessed, "Therefore I hated life," (Ecclesiastes 2:17).

Prosperity Is Simply Having Enough Of God's Provision To Complete His Assignment In Your Life.

Think for a moment. You probably possess more today than at anytime in your whole life. Do you feel more joy than you have ever had in your life? Do you laugh more now than you have ever laughed? Do you enjoy your friendships now more than you ever have? *Be honest with yourself.*

Jesus knew "The eyes of man are never satisfied," (Proverbs 27:20). Some things matter more than money. God will never give you a gift to replace Him.

Never expect money to be enough in your quest for fulfillment.

This is one of the secrets to becoming an Uncommon Achiever.

Our Prayer Together...

"Father, as I achieve Success, please remind me and give me the Wisdom to know that money is not an end...but a means. It cannot bring me happiness...but it can enable me to complete Your instructions for my life. In Jesus' name. Amen."

RECOMMENDED RESOURCES:

MT-14   7 Things a Man Can Do to Build a Strife Free Home (CD/$10)
WCPL-43 7 Things Money Cannot Buy (CD/$10)
WCPL-47 31 Reasons I'm in Love with Jesus (CD/$10)

≈ **18** ≈

DO NOT BE AFRAID TO SHOW YOUR TRUE HEART FEELINGS

Emotions Dictate The World.

"The righteous are bold as a lion," (Proverbs 28:1). Boldness Decides Rulership.

An angered world leader attacks another country. Angry airline employees have a picket line at the airport. A mother whose child is killed by a drunk driver launches a national campaign. Thousands are rallying to stop the abortion of millions of babies.

Feelings do matter in life.

In business, feelings are *contagious.* When a salesman is excited over his product, the customer feels the enthusiasm, and is *influenced* by it.

Jesus was not afraid to express Himself.

When He was infuriated, others knew it. "And the Jews' passover was at hand, and Jesus went up to Jerusalem, And found in the temple those that sold oxen and sheep and doves, and the changers of money sitting: And when he had made a scourge of small cords, he drove them all out of the temple, and the sheep, and the oxen; and poured out the changers' money, and overthrew the tables," (John 2:13-15).

He was *deeply moved* with compassion when He saw multitudes wandering aimlessly without direction. "But when he saw the multitudes, he was moved with compassion on them, because they fainted, and were scattered abroad, as sheep having no shepherd," (Matthew 9:36).

The Bible even records that Jesus wept openly. "And when he was come near, he beheld the city, and wept over it," (Luke 19:41).

I am not speaking about an uncontrollable temper, neither am I referring to someone who sobs and breaks down every time a problem occurs in their life.

Rather, I am asking that you notice that Jesus did not bottle up His emotions. *He was not a robot.* He was *enthusiastic* when He saw a demonstration of faith, He *wept* when He saw unbelief.

Peter, His disciple, was affected by those expressions. The Apostle Paul was set on fire by them. They changed the course of history.

Be bold in expressing your opinions. Feel strongly about things that matter in life. You can be a marvelous influence for good.

You will always be drawn to people who are expressive. Thousands scream at rock concerts, football games and world-championship boxing matches.

Do not be a spectator of life. Get in the arena.

Do not be afraid to show your true feelings...at the appropriate time and place.

This is one of the secrets to becoming an Uncommon Achiever.

❧ **19** ❧

EXUDE GRATITUDE CONTINUOUSLY

Uncommon Achievers Are Thankful.

Appreciative means, "showing appreciation of someone or something; to be grateful."

Ruth was *appreciative.*

It is interesting to note the *reaction* of Ruth when Boaz gave her permission to stay in his field and glean barley. She thanked him warmly. "Then she fell on her face, and bowed herself to the ground, and said unto him, Why have I found grace in thine eyes, that thou shouldest take knowledge of me, seeing I am a stranger? And Boaz answered and said unto her, It hath fully been shewed me, all that thou hast done unto thy mother in law since the death of thine husband: and how thou hast left thy father and thy mother, and the land of thy nativity, and art come unto a people which thou knewest not heretofore," (Ruth 2:10-11).

She continues on in the thirteenth verse, "Then she said, Let me find favour in thy sight, my lord; for that thou hast comforted me, and for that thou hast spoken friendly unto thine handmaid, though I be not like unto one of thine handmaiden." She did not *assume* that this kindness was *owed* her. She really did not even ask for extra favor. She valued the smallest crumb or barley left in her behalf.

Appreciative people have "a magnetism" to them. Their ability to value acts of kindness inspires us and makes us want to perform accordingly.

Years ago, Jessica was a beautiful little nine-year-old girl in Minneapolis, Minnesota. She was so articulate, expressive and appreciative. Every time I did something special for her, she looked up with those big beautiful eyes and the biggest smile you could imagine, and said, "Oh, thank you so very much!" It made her magnetic! It is the attitude of appreciation that makes children so delightful and makes us want to produce for them.

It is often said that Christmas is for children. Now why do we say this when it is celebrated as the birthday of Jesus of Nazareth? Why do we not enjoy Christmas like children?

Children *appreciate.*

They *celebrate* gifts.

Gifts are great events to them.

It is so unfortunate that after some of us receive so many gifts and blessings for so many years, our ability to appreciate seems to deteriorate and diminish dramatically. Work on this in your personal life. Work on this in your home. Do not take for granted that your husband is "supposed to bring home the paycheck." Do not assume that it is "a woman's place" to clean up the house and prepare the meals.

Appreciation of those around you...will make you unforgettable.

Find ways to express your appreciation.

Do it *verbally.* Speak kind words of appreciation.

Do it *privately.* When no one else is around, be

gentle in expressing your true appreciation and gratefulness.

Do it *publicly*. Others need to hear that you know and appreciate what God has blessed you with.

Do it *often*. Not just once a year at a birthday or an anniversary.

Do it *generously*. Go the extra mile when you buy a gift for someone special whom you love and appreciate.

Do it *thoughtfully*. One of my closest friends in Sarasota, Florida, sent me two books recently. What kind of books? The very author that he knows I love to read. He had put *thought* into the purchase of my gifts. He knew what I wanted to read. I have had many people give me books *they* thought I ought to read...very few have purchased for me books that I *wanted* to read.

Do it *quickly*. If someone has blessed your life significantly, do not wait several months or years to express it. Try to establish the habit of responding to an act of kindness within seventy-two hours.

Do it *cheerfully*. When you express your appreciation, do not do it grudgingly as if it is a pain or an effort.

You will become *unforgettable* to every friend in your life.

Exude gratitude continuously.

This is one of the secrets to becoming an Uncommon Achiever.

You Will Only
        Be Remembered In Life
For Two Things:
        The Problems You Solve
Or The Ones You Create.

-MIKE MURDOCK

⚍ **20** ⚍

BECOME KNOWN FOR INTEGRITY

---◆◆◆---

People Talk.

The Biblical story of Ruth is fascinating. Everyone knew about Ruth.

Boaz describes her reputation this way, "And Boaz answered and said unto her, It hath fully been shewed me, all that thou hast done unto thy mother in law since the death of thine husband: and how thou hast left thy father and thy mother, and the land of thy nativity, and art come unto a people which thou knewest not heretofore," (Ruth 2:11).

Later he said, "Blessed be thou of the Lord, my daughter: for thou hast shewed more kindness in the latter end than at the beginning, inasmuch as thou followedst not young men, whether poor or rich. And now, my daughter, fear not; I will do to thee all that thou requirest: for all the city of my people doth know that thou art a virtuous woman," (Ruth 3:10-11).

*People talk...*good things and bad things...false accusations and current assessments.

You Will Only Be Remembered In Life For Two Things: The Problems You Solve Or The Ones You Create.

People spoke well of Ruth. Her sacrificial attitude and dedication to preserving and maintaining the life of her widowed mother-in-law was a known fact in the community. Obviously, she had not even dated or bonded with any of the young men in the city—poor or rich. Her *total focus* was on Naomi.

Character is a choice.

This had registered heavily in the heart and mind of Boaz who did not hesitate to respond to her pursuit of a relationship with him.

Are others able to commend you? "Let another man praise thee, and not thine own mouth; a stranger, and not thine own lips," (Proverbs 27:2).

Reputation is more powerful than money. "A good name is rather to be chosen than great riches, and loving favour rather than silver and gold," (Proverbs 22:1).

A good name is more magnetic than a strong fragrance. "A good name is better than precious ointment; and the day of death than the day of one's birth," (Ecclesiastes 7:1).

Several years ago, I arrived at the house of a young lady to take her to supper. As we were driving to the restaurant she remarked, "I had another date planned tonight, but I told him I had to visit a relative in the hospital."

She had lied. *It sickened me.* I had been excited about establishing a relationship with her only to find out within minutes that falsehood came naturally and easily to her. Obviously, I would be the next victim on her list. It was the first and last date I had with her.

Whatever it takes...develop integrity.

Focus on it. Carefully examine each word and sentence that comes from your lips. Never say anything insincere. Refuse to brag on someone's singing if it is untrue. Do not say things merely to encourage others. "Recompense to no man evil for evil. Provide things honest in the sight of all men," (Romans 12:17).

The *compassion* of Ruth was known.

Observe how a woman speaks to her mother. Note well how a man treats his mother. Also, observe how he reacts to the struggle and heartaches of the unfortunate.

Ruth's *purity* and *virtue* were known. Admittedly, many false accusations are hurled these days. Good people have been stained through vindictive and violent people. Remember Potiphar's wife? (See Genesis 39:7-20.) Joseph is not the only story where someone, who has walked totally before the Lord, had his reputation devastated by those they had resisted or ignored.

However, the entire town knew of Ruth's obsession to serve, as well as her kindness to her mother-in-law. *It was said that she treated her mother-in-law better than seven sons would treat a mother.* That kind of reputation is almost unheard of today.

This does not mean you have to advertise all your good deeds. It is not important that you announce to the world all your acts of kindness and mercy. Somehow, God has a way of "letting your integrity be made known."

What you are...will eventually be exposed and known. Yes, these are marvelous qualities that make you unforgettable.

Become known for integrity.

This is one of the secrets to becoming an Uncommon Achiever.

False Accusation Is The Last Step Before Supernatural Promotion.

-MIKE MURDOCK

❧ 21 ❧

REFUSE TO BE DISCOURAGED WHEN OTHERS MISJUDGE YOUR MOTIVES

Everyone Has Been Misjudged.

You will always have an adversary. "The words of the wicked are to lie in wait for blood: but the mouth of the upright shall deliver them," (Proverbs 12:6).

When a minister speaks on prosperity, he *risks* being accused of greed. When he prays for the sick, he *risks* being called a fraud and a fake.

Your own family may misjudge your motives. Any person who carries out instructions for you may misjudge your actions.

Your boss might misread you. Customers may doubt your sincerity.

Do not be discouraged. Take the time to discuss your position with those who appear genuinely sincere. Do not waste your time and energy on those who are merely stirring up conflict.

Jesus was constantly misjudged by others. Pharisees accused Him of even being possessed by evil spirits. "But when the Pharisees heard it, they said, This fellow doth not cast out devils, but by Beelzebub the prince of the devils," (Matthew 12:24).

Let me make a few suggestions. When you speak

to others, be concise. Be bold but very distinct in what you say. Do not leave room for misunderstandings when possible.

Always be where you are. When you are in conversation with someone, totally focus on that conversation. Shut out everything else. When you totally focus on what you are saying and hearing, you do not have to reflect later with regret about that conversation. This can prevent unnecessary misjudgment.

Every extraordinary Achiever has been misjudged. People laughed over the thought of a *horseless carriage.* Others sneered when the *telephone* was invented.

Your success is on the other side of scorn and false accusations.

False Accusation Is The Last Stage Before Supernatural Promotion.

Refuse to be discouraged when others misjudge you.

This is one of the secrets to becoming an Uncommon Achiever.

Our Prayer Together...

"Father, thank You for redeeming situations in which others are critical or falsely accuse me. I rest in knowing that as I pattern myself after Jesus in ignoring my accusers, I will reach the other side of adversity—success. In Jesus' name. Amen."

RECOMMENDED RESOURCES:
B-19   Seeds of Wisdom on Warfare (32 pages/$3)
B-21   Seeds of Wisdom on Adversity (32 pages/$3)
TS-03   How To Walk Through Fire And Not Be Burned
         (6 tapes/$30)
WCPL-22 When Your Goliath Arrives (CD/$10)

∾ 22 ∾

DEVELOP CONFIDENCE IN YOUR DIFFERENCE

You Are Important.

Some do not qualify for your time nor energy. "Give not that which is holy unto the dogs, neither cast ye your pearls before swine, lest they trample them under their feet, and turn again and rend you," (Matthew 7:6).

You have nothing to prove to anyone.

You are the offspring of a remarkable Creator.

You have the mind of Christ.

Your gifts and talents have been placed within you. *Find what they are. Celebrate them.* Find ways to use those gifts to improve others and help them achieve their dreams and goals.

Never, never exhaust and waste your energies trying to prove something to somebody else. *Go Where You Are Celebrated Instead Of Where You Are Tolerated.*

Your worth must be discerned.

Jesus knew this. Satan tempted Him. "If thou be the Son of God, command that these stones be made bread," (Matthew 4:3).

Jesus unstopped deaf ears. He opened blind eyes. He made the lame to walk. The dead were raised. Sinners were changed.

Yet, the jeers of the doubters continued to scream into His ears at His crucifixion, "And saying, Thou that destroyest the temple, and buildest it in three days, save thyself. If thou be the Son of God, come down from the cross," (Matthew 27:40).

What was Jesus' reaction? *He was confident of His worth. He knew His purpose.* He refused to let the taunts of ignorant men change His plans.

You are not responsible for anything but an honest effort to please God. *Keep focused.*

Develop Confidence In Your Difference.

This is one of the secrets to becoming an Uncommon Achiever.

Our Prayer Together...

"Father, I thank You for not making me responsible for anything but an honest effort to please You. Help me to remember that I do not find my value in what others think of me, but in what You think of me. In Jesus' name. Amen."

≈ 23 ≈

REMEMBER THAT GOD IS VERY AWARE OF THE HIDDEN GREATNESS WITHIN YOU OTHERS DO NOT YET DISCERN

<hr/>

Something Incredible Is Inside You.

The Price God Was Willing To Pay Reveals The Worth Of The Product He Saw.

Your *Assignment* was decided in your mother's womb. "Before I formed thee in the belly I knew thee; and before thou camest forth out of the womb I sanctified thee, and I ordained thee a prophet unto the nations," (Jeremiah 1:5). God knows it. He created you. He has known the invisible purpose for which you were created.

You are not an accident waiting to happen. "I will praise Thee; for I am fearfully and wonderfully made: marvellous are Thy works; and that my soul knoweth right well," (Psalm 139:14).

Everything inside you is known, treasured and intended for full use by your Creator. "My substance was not hid from Thee, when I was made in secret, and curiously wrought in the lowest parts of the earth," (Psalm 139:15).

Your flaws do not necessarily prevent God from using you. They exist to motivate your pursuit of Him.

"Thine eyes did see my substance, yet being unperfect; and in thy book all my members were written, which in continuance were fashioned, when as yet there was none of them," (Psalm 139:16).

Your very existence excites God. "How precious also are Thy thoughts unto me, O God! how great is the sum of them! If I should count them, they are more in number than the sand: when I awake, I am still with Thee," (Psalm 139:17-18).

Picture an author exultant over his book. *The book exists.* The author created it. He is excited about it whether anyone else is or not. Imagine a composer, exhilarated over a completed song. He knew its beginning and its ending. Its very presence excites him.

Your very presence energizes God. He saw your beginning and the desired conclusion. "For Thou hast created all things, and for Thy pleasure they are and were created," (Revelation 4:11).

God is looking at something within you that you have never seen. "For man looketh on the outward appearance, but the Lord looketh on the heart," (1 Samuel 16:7).

God is looking at something you contain that you have not yet discovered. "For as the heavens are higher than the earth, so are My ways higher than your ways, and My thoughts than your thoughts," (Isaiah 55:9).

God will tell you secrets that satan will never hear. *God is looking at something inside you that satan cannot even discern.* (Read Job 1-3.)

His mercies are not wasted on you. He has big plans. His forgiveness is not futile. You are becoming a monument and trophy of His grace. "For we are His workmanship, created in Christ Jesus unto good works," (Ephesians 2:10).

God boasts about you to every demon. (See Job 1:8.)

You may be looking at your *beginning.*
God is looking at your *end.*
You may be obsessed with your *flaws.*
God is obsessed with your *future.*
You may be focusing on your *enemies.*
God is focusing on your *eventuality.*

God is not *waiting* for you to become your Assignment. He is awaiting your *discovery* of it.

Don't bond with those who have not discovered what is within you. Their focus is different. Their conclusions are inaccurate.

Stay in the presence of the One that created you. You will always feel confident about yourself when you stay in His presence. He is looking at something in you that is remarkable. He planted something within you while you were yet in your mother's womb. (See Jeremiah 1:5.)

David understood this. King Saul and his brothers saw *brashness;* The Holy Spirit saw *boldness.* His brothers saw *anger;* God saw a *sense of justice.* (See 1 Samuel 17:26-31.)

Joseph understood this. His brothers saw *pride.* God saw *thankfulness.* The brothers saw *rivalry;* God saw a *weapon.* (See Genesis 37:4-11.)

That is why the opinions and observations of others are not your foundation for greatness. Stop pursuing their conclusions. God is looking at something inside you that they *cannot see, refuse* to see and may *never* see.

The brothers of Jesus did not grasp His divinity. (See Matthew 12:47-50.)

The brothers of Joseph misinterpreted him.

The brothers of David saw a mere shepherd boy.

The friends of Job could not discern the satanic scenario before his crisis. (See Job 1:8-12.)

Haman could not even discern the nationality of Esther! (See Esther 7:3-6.) *Only fools ignore the preferences of the king.*

Few are ever accurate in their assessment of you.

Your flaws are *much less* than they imagine.

Your greatness is *far greater* than they discern.

The Holy Spirit Is The Only Person Capable Of Being Completely Satisfied With You.

The Holy Spirit is the only One Who has accurately assessed your future, your ingredients and the willingness of your heart to become great. That is why He keeps reaching, pursuing and developing you in the midst of every attack and crisis.

He never *gives up* on you, The Seeker.

He never *quits* looking at you, The Pursuer.

He never *changes* His plans toward you.

He never *quits* believing in your future.

He has decided the conclusion and is only awaiting your discovery of it.

God Sees Something In You That Others Do Not See.

*Remember this continuously...*God is seeing something inside you that keeps Him excited and involved. "Then Samuel took the horn of oil, and anointed him in the midst of his brethren: and the Spirit of the Lord came upon David from that day forward," (1 Samuel 16:13).

Remember That God Is Very Aware Of The Hidden Greatness Within You Others Do Not Yet Discern.

This is one of the secrets to becoming an Uncommon Achiever.

RECOMMENDED RESOURCES:
WCPL-40   Secrets in Discerning the Invisible Gifts Within You
(CD/$10)
You Will Love Our Website...! www.TheWisdomCenter.tv

Greatness Is Simply
Fulfilling God's
Expectations Of You.

-MIKE MURDOCK

24

ALWAYS CLOSE DOORS GENTLY

Relationships Do Not Always Last Forever.

It is therefore important to exit every door of friendship properly. You cannot enter the next season of your life with joy unless you exit your present season correctly.

Jesus *finished* His work on earth. He cried out from the cross, "It is finished!" (See John 19:30.) Salvation was complete. Redemption had taken place. He had paid the price for the sins of man. Three days later, the resurrection would take place. He would return to the Father where He would make intercession for you and me. He finished *properly...with* the approval of the Father.

Solomon *finished* the temple. It was an incredible feat. Some value his temple today at over $500 billion dollars. He was respected, pursued and celebrated. He *completed* what he started. (See 2 Chronicles 7:11.)

Greatness Is Simply Fulfilling God's Expectations Of You.

Paul *finished* his race. He fought a good fight, kept his course and finished the race. He was a success in the eyes of God. He made his exit from his earthly ministry with grace, passion and dignity. (See 2 Timothy 4:7.)

Your life is a collection of *Beginnings.*

It is also a collection of *Exits.*

You will not stay in your present job forever. You will someday leave your present position. Your supervisor today could be another acquaintance in your life, next year. Close the relationship with dignity.

8 Keys To Remember When A Relationship Is Ending

1. *Close Every Door Gently.* Do not slam doors. Do not kick doors. Do not yell at doors. They are doors through which you may need to return again in the future. The attitude of your exit determines if you can ever walk back through that door again. "A soft answer turneth away wrath: but grievous words stir up anger," (Proverbs 15:1).

2. *Close Doors With Forgiveness.* Unforgiveness is poisonous. It is the cancer that will destroy you from within. Release others to God. Permit *Him* to do the penalizing or correcting. Like Joseph, recognize that the ultimate plan of God will bring your promotion. (See Romans 8:28.)

3. *Close The Doors With Kindness.* If your fiancee leaves you with cutting and bitter words, thank The Holy Spirit for salvaging you. Perhaps she was not your *Proverbs 31 Woman* after all. "In her tongue is the law of kindness," (Proverbs 31:26).

4. *Close Every Door With Promises Fulfilled.* Do not leave your job until you have finished what you promised. Complete every vow...*whatever* the cost. Integrity is easy to test. Simply ask yourself, "Did I fulfill my promise?" (Read Ecclesiastes 5:4-5.)

When people lose you in the forest of words, apply this principle of *vow fulfillment*. Forget the blaming, complaining and accusations. This principle reveals everything you need to know about another.

5.   *Close Every Door With Integrity.* Few will do it. People are rarely angry for the reason they tell you. Much is never discussed. The trap of deception is deadly. It begins when you deceive *yourself,* followed by those around you. Always be honest to others about the reason for the doors closing. It is not necessary to give *every* detail. It *is* important that the details you give are *accurate.*

6.   *Close Every Door With Courage.* It is not always easy to close a door that The Holy Spirit requires. So, closing that door may require uncommon courage in facing the future without that person. Remember The Precious Holy Spirit will never leave you nor forsake you. (See John 14:16.) He *opens* doors. He *closes* doors. He is *The Bridge...*to every person in your future.

7.   *Close Every Door With Expectation Of Promotion.* "For promotion cometh neither from the east, nor from the west, nor from the south. But God is the judge: he putteth down one, and setteth up another," (Psalm 75:6-7).

8.   *Close Every Door By The Timing Of The Holy Spirit.* Do not close it in a fit of anger. Do not close the door because of a misunderstanding that erupts. Do not close it just because someone *recommends* that you exit. *Know the timing of God.*

A young man sat in my kitchen a few weeks ago. I was quite concerned. He wanted a position in my ministry. I asked him about his relationship with his previous boss, my preacher friend. He avoided the issue continually. In fact, I had to ask him the question four or five times before I got a partial answer. At the end of the conversation, he explained his financial dilemma. He had left a job before ever securing another one. I explained to him how *foolish* this was. If God were moving him, He would tell him the place he was to go.

When God told Elijah to leave the brook, Zarephath was scheduled. (See 1 Kings 17.)

When the Israelites left Egypt, Canaan was their determined destination. (See Exodus 13.)

God always brings you out of a place to bring you into another place. So, close every door with God's timing. When you close doors gently, news will travel...*good news.*

Always Close Doors Gently.

This is one of the secrets to becoming an Uncommon Achiever.

RECOMMENDED RESOURCES:
WCPL-11 7 Keys to Mastering Stress, Vols. 1-2 (2 CDs/$15)
WCPL-15 Hidden Secrets in Protecting Good Relationships (CD/$10)
WCPL-17 The Law of Protocol and The Reward It Creates (CD/$10)
WCPL-26 7 Kinds of People You Cannot Help (CD/$10)
WCPL-27 The Hidden Power of Right Words (CD/$10)
WCPL-36 The High Price of Wrong People In Your Life (CD/$10)

⤳ 25 ⤳

EMBRACE THE CORRECTION OF OTHER UNCOMMON ACHIEVERS

⟹⟾

God Assigns Deliverers.

An Uncommon Future Requires An Uncommon Mentor.

Moses was assigned to lead the Israelites out of Egypt. Elijah was sent to the widow of Zaraphath to help her use her faith.

If you are sick...*look* for the man of God who believes in healing.

If you are having financial problems...*look* for the man of God who believes in prosperity.

No one fails alone. If you fail, it will be because you chose to ignore those God assigned to help you.

Recognize messengers from God.

When Satan Wants To Destroy You, He Puts A Person Into Your Life. When God Wants To Bless You, He Brings A Person Into Your Life. Recognize them. Whether they are packaged like a John the Baptist in a loincloth of camel's hair, or in the silk robes of King Solomon.

Your reaction to a man or woman of God is carefully documented by God. When God talks to you, it is often through the spiritual leaders in your life. *Do not ignore them.* "He that receiveth a prophet in the name of a prophet shall receive a prophet's reward; and he that receiveth a righteous man in the name of a righteous man shall receive a righteous man's reward," (Matthew 10:41).

Embrace The Correction Of Other Uncommon Achievers.

This is one of the secrets to becoming an Uncommon Achiever.

⪧ 26 ⪦

BECOME AN ENEMY TO YOUR WEAKNESS

Never Trivialize Your Weakness.

An Unconquered Weakness Always Births A Tragedy.

The cost is too high.

I have been in full-time ministry for over 40 years and watched incredible, powerful and extraordinary men *fall* from their thrones into ashes...good men...articulate men...brilliant men.

A *tiny weakness* began to eat its way into their lives like a small cancer. Greed, lust, lying, prayerlessness, or gossip grew until that weakness became a raging inferno. The small puppy became a rabid monster.

Anything Permitted Increases.

Your weakness may presently be at the embryonic state...perhaps the size of an acorn. Nobody else can see it yet. You may even joke about it. You *cannot* afford to play with a weakness in your life.

You see, when you are not victorious, you will become miserable. That misery creates agitation. That agitation will cause you to lash out at those you love, thus destroying the very foundation of your life.

40 Facts About Your Weakness

1. *The War Of Your Life Is Between Your Strength And Your Weakness.* (See Galatians 5:17.)

2. *Everyone Has A Weakness.* "For all have sinned," (Romans 3:23).

3. *Your Weakness Will Bond You With The Wrong People.* Remember Samson and Delilah? (See Judges 16:4-20.)

4. *Your Weakness Can Multiply.* "...a little leaven leaventh the whole lump?" (1 Corinthians 5:6).

5. *Your Weakness Should Be Confronted When It First Emerges At Its Early Sign Of Exposure.*

6. *Your Weakness Separates You From The Right People.* Adam withdrew from God in the Garden after he sinned. (See Genesis 3:8.)

7. *Few Will Confront Their Weakness With The Proper Weaponry, The Word Of God.* "Wherewithal shall a young man cleanse his way? by taking heed thereto according to Thy Word," (Psalm 119:9).

8. *Your Weakness Can Emerge At Any Time In Your Life, Including Your Closing Years.* "Cast me not off in the time of old age; forsake me not when my strength faileth," (Psalm 71:9).

9. *Your Weakness Is The Entry Point For Satan And Demonic Spirits.* Satan entered Judas. (See Luke 22:3.)

10. *Your Weakness Cannot Be Overcome With Humanism, Human Philosophy, Explanations, Or Self Will Power.* If your weakness could be overcome by yourself, the blood of Jesus is powerless and The Holy Spirit is unnecessary. "But ye shall receive power, after that the Holy Ghost is come upon you," (Acts 1:8).

11. *Satan Will Invest Whatever Time Is Necessary To Nurture A Small Weakness Into A Raging Wolf That Destroys You.* Keep resisting. (See Matthew 4:3-10.)

12. *Your Weakness Does Not Necessarily Have To Be Confessed To Everybody.* You must admit it to yourself and to your Heavenly Father though. (See Psalm 34:18, James 5:16.)

13. *Your Heavenly Father Is Fully Aware Of Your Weakness.* It matters to Him. He reaches out to you to annihilate it. "For He remembered that they were but flesh; a wind that passeth away, and cometh not again," (Psalm 78:39, see also Psalm 103:13).

14. *Somebody Is Assigned By Hell To Fuel And Strengthen Your Weakness.* Delilah was sent by satan to destroy Samson. (See Judges 16:4-5.)

15. *The Lives And Futures Of Those You Love Are Awaiting Your Overcoming And Triumph Over Your Weakness.* Your victory means victory for them!

When David killed Goliath, the entire nation of Israel changed seasons. Your family is sitting in fear of their own weaknesses that can destroy them. They will be strengthened when they see you victorious over your weakness. (See 1 Samuel 17:52-53.)

16. *Your Weakness Searches For Every Opportunity To Grow.* (See Matthew 6:22-23.)

17. *Your Weakness Will Embrace And Seize Any Friendship That Permits It, Allows It To Exist And Finds It Tolerable.*

18. *What Others May Not Consider A Weakness, God Knows Is Your Weakness.* Your conscience confirms it, too.

19. *Every Weakness Grows.* It *cannot* stay the

same. It is being fed and nourished or destroyed and starved. "Your glorying is not good. Know ye not that a little leaven leaveneth the whole lump?" (1 Corinthians 5:6).

20. *You Must Starve Your Weakness A Day At A Time.* Make no room for the flesh. (See Romans 13:14.)

21. *Your Weakness Will Not Remain In You Alone But Will Move Towards Others And Infect Those Around You.* It will become bigger and bigger, stronger and stronger. It considers you, your dreams and future to be its greatest enemy.

22. *Your Weakness Hates Your Strengths.* You see, your strengths are a threat to your weakness.

23. *Your Weakness Does Not Want To Stay Small.*

24. *Your Weakness Does Not Want To Remain Insignificant.* It *craves* expression.

25. *Your Weakness Will Become Angry When It Is Ignored.*

26. *Your Weakness Has A Will Of Its Own.* "I find then a law, that, when I would do good, evil is present with me," (Romans 7:21).

27. *Your Weakness Has An Agenda, A Plan To Take Over Your Life And Sabotage It.* "Then when lust hath conceived, it bringeth forth sin: and sin, when it is finished, bringeth forth death," (James 1:15).

28. *Your Weakness Despises The Exploits And Accomplishments Of Your Strength.* (See Judges 16:6).

29. *Your Weakness Must Be Destroyed, Not Tolerated Or Enjoyed Occasionally.* (See 1 Samuel 15:7-10).

30. *God Will Permit You To Enjoy Many*

Victories. This is true even while your weakness is in its beginning stages. He is long-suffering and merciful. He gives you chance after chance, opportunity after opportunity to repent and reach for deliverance. Jesus cried, "How often would I have gathered thy children together, even as a hen gathereth her chickens under her wings, and ye would not!" (Matthew 23:37).

31. *When You Justify Your Weakness, It Laughs With Glee Knowing That In Due Time It Will Displace A Strength In Your Life.*

32. *Your Weakness Can Only Be Overcome By The Word Of God In Your Life When You Confront It.* Satan attempts to camouflage your weakness, wrapping it in acceptable vocabulary. Jesus used the Word as a weapon. (See Matthew 4:1-11.)

33. *God Wants To Grow Your Strength And Destroy Your Weakness.* "Likewise reckon ye also yourselves to be dead indeed unto sin, but alive unto God through Jesus Christ our Lord," (Romans 6:11).

34. *Your Weakness Has Cousins.* It will not rest until every one of them come to visit and take up a void in your life. The adultery of David birthed the murder of Uriah. (See 2 Samuel 11:1-17.)

35. *Nobody Has Merely One Weakness.* Your strongest weakness invites another one to come and visit.

36. *Your Victory Over Your Weakness Will Unlock Victories For Others.* It is so even if they are unaware of your weakness.

37. *Your Weakness Is Always An Enemy To Thankfulness.* You see, you are never thankful for a weakness. Weakness is unappreciated. It reacts

vehemently and begins a relentless journey to choke out any sign of thankfulness. It knows you hate it. It never receives the praise, adoration and recognition that your strength receives.

38. *God Makes Every Effort To Reveal Your Weakness To You Before It Destroys You.* "And the Lord said, Simon, Simon, behold, Satan hath desired to have you, that he may sift you as wheat," (Luke 22:31).

39. *It Is Possible To Know And Recognize Your Own Weakness Before Others Know It.* Peter discovered this. (See Matthew 26:33-35, 73-75.)

40. *Overcoming Your Weakness Brings Incredible Rewards For All Eternity.* (See Revelation 3.)

Your weakness is not a whimpering puppy to be fed when hungry. Your weakness is a deadly, rabid wolf to be *despised, rejected* and *destroyed.*

Do not make friends with your weakness. Do not bond with it.

The Presence Of God Is The Only Place Your Weakness Will Die.

Become an enemy to your weakness.

This is one of the secrets to becoming an Uncommon Achiever.

≈ 27 ≈

BECOME A PROTEGÉ TO AN UNCOMMON MENTOR

━━━━➤○⋖━━━━

A Mentor Is A Trusted Teacher.

An Uncommon Future Requires An Uncommon Mentor.

Your mentor sees your future *before* you do.

Mentors are not necessarily cheerleaders. A mentor is a *coach*. Their role is not merely to confirm what you are doing correctly. Their goal is to correct you and prevent you from making a mistake.

There are two ways to learn:

1. Mistakes.
2. Mentors.

Mentorship Is Wisdom Without The Pain.

Mentorship Is Success Without The Wait.

In Scriptures, Ruth is a remarkable example of a protegé.

Ruth had not remarried when she followed her mother-in-law, Naomi, back to Bethlehem.

She worked hard. One day, Naomi *expressed* that it was time for Ruth to have a husband in her life. She *advised* her to go to the threshing floor where Boaz worked every night. Naomi *knew* the habits of extraordinary men.

Great Men Simply Have Great Habits.

She *advised* Ruth to avoid discussions with him while he was having supper or even working. She *instructed* Ruth that there would be an appropriate time that Boaz would awaken, see her and discuss the details related to their relationship.

Ruth *listened.* She *followed* the instructions. History records the incredible parade of benefits that followed.

Ruth was *teachable.* Boaz had instructed her to restrict her work and the gathering of food to his fields alone and not go into other fields. Naomi had given the same instructions. Ruth *followed* them.

Hearing advice is not the key to success.

Applying good advice is the key to extraordinary success.

One of my pastor friends has had remarkable success in his ministry. He shared with me an important key concerning counseling.

"Mike, I refuse to counsel anyone personally until they have sat in every single service in which I have ministered for a period of six weeks. If their questions and problems have not been resolved through my teaching over a six-week period, I will schedule a personal counseling session with them. In that session, I give specific instructions to be followed. If they do not follow those instructions, I refuse to give a second counseling session. It is a waste of my time and theirs, if they refuse to implement the Wisdom I impart."

You can predict the success of someone by their ability to follow instructions.

The Instruction You Follow Determines The Future You Create.

I am praying that God returns a real respect for the elderly of our generation. Some older women in our generation have more insight and Wisdom in their little finger than many young girls will have within the next twenty years of their lives.

Elisha *sat* at the feet of Elijah.

Timothy *sat* at the feet of Paul.

Esther *listened* to Mordecai and the eunuch who advised her.

Joshua *sat* at the feet of Moses.

Your mentor foresees problems you cannot see coming.

Your Goals Decide Your Mentors.

Are you planning to enter the field of real estate? Find the most successful and productive realtor within one-hundred miles. Establish a friendship. Become their protegé.

Do you long for a useful ministry? Find a man or woman of God to serve. Carry their briefcase. Shine their shoes. Babysit their children. Clean their house. Wash their car. *Do whatever is necessary to access their anointing, connect with their climate and attach yourself to their atmosphere.*

Whatever is growing in your mentor will begin to grow within you.

Whatever they have decided to starve will die within you.

Ruth *applied* good advice when she heard it. It made her unforgettable.

5 Facts About Mentorship

1. *You Will Usually Have More Than One Mentor In Your Life.* Financial, spiritual and academic Mentors exist everywhere.

2. *Different Kinds Of Mentorships Exist.* Some

of us are mentored through tapes, books and relation-ships. However, there can always be a primary Mentor who remains with you throughout your life.

My father is the most important Mentor in my daily life. For many years I struggled to impress him rather than to receive from him. I wanted him to celebrate my discoveries rather than sit and absorb *his* discoveries. After understanding mentorship, now I learn more from him in a single day than I used to learn in a year. Pursue, cherish and protect your gift from God...*your Mentor.*

3. *Respect And Protect The Access Your Mentor Permits You.* He will not always be there. You must face some battles alone. So drink deeply from his well now while you have access.

4. *Treasure Any Invitation For Private Discussion With Your Mentor.* The presence of others changes the level of intimacy and information. When I am alone with my father, I receive much more than I do when others are present. The information is more specific...exact...precise...*just for me.* The thoughts and opinions of others present often dilute and even weaken the impartation.

5. *Your Mentor Often Discerns Whether You Discern His Worth Or Not.* No words need to be spoken. Flattering words are unnecessary. Persuasive words do not matter. When you are in the presence of someone who truly respects what you know, you detect it instantly.

The Pursuit Of The Mentor Reveals The Passion Of The Protegé.

Become A Protegé To An Uncommon Mentor.

This is one of the secrets to becoming an Uncommon Achiever.

∾ 28 ∾

STAY AWARE OF THE UNSPOKEN AGENDA OF OTHERS

❯▰◦▰❮

Respect The Responsibilities Of Another.

I had finished a two-day School of The Holy Spirit up north. It had been a glorious two days. The presence of God was so powerful. I loved being with my friends and partners, as always.

However, due to the airline schedule, I had to leave thirty minutes earlier than planned. Another minister was going to finish the session for me. Because of the airline schedule, two flights were necessary and would let me arrive at my destination approximately at 1:00 a.m. My schedule was hectic. In fact, I would barely make the church where I was scheduled. I announced to everyone present that my plane schedule was tight. I would be unable to stay afterwards for any additional conversation.

Yet, as I was rushing toward the door with my briefcase, my associate by my side, five to seven people stopped me. Standing in front of me, they insisted that I autograph my books. Some insisted that I hear about an experience they had had.

Each one of them *totally ignored my own schedule.* They had no concern whatsoever.

Did they love me? Possibly. But, they really loved *themselves.* Their only obsession was to get something *they* wanted, regardless of the toll it took on me. My needs meant nothing. My own schedule was unimportant to them.

The Holy Spirit is always offended by such insensitivity and uncaring for others, "In honour preferring one another," (Romans 12:10).

Always make sure your time with someone is appropriate for their schedule. (See Ecclesiastes 3:1-8.)

Reject manipulating, intimidating and abusive words. Statements like, "You never take time for me," is simply an attempt to intimidate you. Statements like, "You always have time for everyone else!" is *victim* vocabulary. This kind of person has no true regard for others. They are obsessed with themselves. You cannot give them enough time or attention to satisfy them.

Always mark those who show disregard and disrespect for your time, the most precious gift God gave you.

Those Who Do Not Respect Your Time Will Not Respect Your Wisdom Either.

When you honor the schedule of others, favor will follow.

This is one of the secrets to becoming an Uncommon Achiever.

RECOMMENDED RESOURCES:
TS-24   31 Secrets of The Uncommon Problem-Solver
          (6 tapes/$30)

≈ 29 ≈

VIEW THE VARIATION IN PERSONALITIES AS A NECESSARY INGREDIENT FOR YOUR PERSONAL SUCCESS

Greatness Is Everywhere.

Your Reaction To Greatness Reveals Your Humility.

"The heart of the prudent getteth knowledge; and the ear of the wise seeketh knowledge," (Proverbs 18:15).

People have different contributions. I believe you need different kinds of input into your life. Someone needs what you possess. You need something that they can contribute to you. You are the sum total of your experiences.

Personalities differ. Each person around you contains a different body of knowledge. It is up to you to "drop your pail in their well," and draw it out. "Where no counsel is, the people fall: but in the multitude of counsellors there is safety," (Proverbs 11:14).

*Look at those who surrounded Jesus...*a tax collector...a physician...a fisherman...a woman who had been possessed with seven devils.

Some were poor. Some were wealthy. Some were

very energetic while others were passive. Some were explosive like Peter. Others, like James, were logical.

Be willing to listen to others. Everyone sees through different eyes. They feel with different hearts. They hear through different ears. *Someone knows something that you should know.* You will not discover it until you take the time to stop and hear them out. *One piece of information can turn a failure into a success.* Great decisions are products of great thoughts.

Successful people treasure worthy friendships. Names are vital. Building a significant rolodex or address book is a must. Keep in touch regularly with those who love you.

Every successful pastor knows the importance of a name. That is why visitor cards are given out at most services. Receptions where greeters meet newcomers are held every Sunday morning. Millions of dollars are spent on television programs, radio broadcasts and newspaper ads—because of the name of those who are important to their vision.

Every successful businessman knows the importance of a single name. Listen to Ron Popeil, a multimillionaire who has enjoyed great success. "One of the mandates at Ronco, besides quality of innovation, is this: A name, address and phone number are worth gold. We always capture a telephone number in addition to the name and address of a customer, because those items are very common, very valuable," (page 219, *The Salesman Of the Century*).

Avoid keeping names and addresses in many different places.

Keep one Master Address Book.

My dentist's name is kept under "D." When I want to buy carpet, I look under "C" where I have placed the business card of a local carpet store.

Think of everyone around you as a potential problem-solver for your life. Treasure your access to them. When you receive a business card, place it under the divider most appropriate. For instance, if you meet Mr. Sam Jones who sells automobiles, do not put his business card under "J" for Jones. You will not remember it a year later. Place his business card under "A" for automobiles.

Friendships are too precious to lose. They cost too much to treat lightly. I once read where one of our U.S. presidents had 7,500 names in his rolodex. He loved people. He valued people. He knew the importance of a name.

Build a master Address Book of those who truly matter to your life.

Pay any price to stay connected to extraordinary people.

Jesus networked.

Network with people of all backgrounds.

This is one of the secrets to becoming an Uncommon Achiever.

Our Prayer Together...

"I realize, Lord, that Your creation is filled with many extraordinary and different people. Give me the Wisdom and ability to recognize that who I spend my time with is time invested in my success. In Jesus' name. Amen."

Successful Men
Do Daily
What Unsuccessful Men
Do Occasionally.

-MIKE MURDOCK

☙ **30** ☙

CREATE A CUSTOMIZED TRAINING PROGRAM FOR THE DREAM TEAM YOU ARE DEVELOPING AROUND YOU

You Will Always Remember What You Teach.

Willingly mentor the inexperienced around you. "Give instruction to a wise man, and he will be yet wiser: teach a just man, and he will increase in learning," (Proverbs 9:9).

Someone has said that you do not learn anything when you talk. You only learn when you listen. That is an inaccurate concept. Some of my greatest thoughts and ideas have surfaced while I was teaching others.

It is very important that you mentor someone. *Train them.* Teach them what you know. Especially those over whom you have authority...any person who is carrying out an instruction for you...employees, children or whoever.

Successful businesses have employees who are informed, well-trained and confident about carrying out their instructions. This takes time. It takes energy. It requires great patience.

Every song needs a singer. Every Achiever needs motivation. Every student needs a teacher.

Jesus was a master teacher. He taught thousands at a time. Sometimes, He sat with His twelve disciples and fed information into them. He kept them motivated, influenced and inspired.

He taught them about prayer (Matthew 26:36-46).

He taught them about Heaven (John 14:2-4).

He taught them about hell (Luke 16:20-31).

He educated His staff on many topics including His death, giving and relationships.

Jesus taught in synagogues (Luke 13:10). He also taught in the villages (Mark 6:6).

Here is the point. None of us were born with great knowledge. You *became* what you are. You *discovered* what you know. It took time, energy and learning.

Your staff will not know everything. They may not see what you see. They may not feel what you feel. They may not have discovered what you have.

You must invest time to nurture their vision, their product knowledge and the rewards you want them to pursue.

You need good people around you. You need *inspired* people around you. You need *informed* people around you. You may be their *only* source for information and motivation.

Jesus educated His staff. Jesus constantly motivated the people He led by showing them the future of their present commitment (Mark 10:29-30).

My Greatest Ministry Turning Point came when I created 80 Training Videos and DVD's...personally taught to my Team. I terminated 5 employees, saved over $300,000...and imparted my vision into those *qualified to be a part of...The Wisdom Center.*

Take the time to train others.

This is one of the secrets to becoming an Uncommon Achiever.

RECOMMENDED RESOURCES:

WCPL-73 The Mystery and The Miracle of Mentorship
(CD/$10)

WCPL-76 How to Communicate Effectively With People
(CD/$10)

All Men Fall,
The Great Ones
Get Back Up.

-MIKE MURDOCK

≈ 31 ≈

GIVE THOSE WHO FAIL A CHANCE TO TRY AGAIN

━━━━━▶-◉-◀━━━━━

Everybody Makes Mistakes.
All Men Fall, The Great Ones Get Back Up.
Everybody deserves the chance to change.
Allow them to do so.

When pressure increases, those around you are affected and influenced. Their stress can affect you. The constant demands of others often births impatience and mistakes. During these moments, *your mercy is necessary.*

Wrong words are often blurted out.
Inaccurate assessments are made.
Wrong decisions are made.
Always Allow Others Room To Turn Around.

Think back upon your own life. Many frustrations drove you to that moment of indiscretion, those cutting words and angry outbursts.

Greatness Is Not The Absence Of A Flaw—But The Willingness To Overcome It.

Allow forgiveness.

Don't force others to live by their past bad decisions. Whatever you sow will come back to you a hundred times. So give them space to come back into the relationship with dignity. Jesus taught it. "Blessed are the merciful: for they shall obtain mercy," (Matthew 5:7).

Forgive them 490 times. "Then came Peter to him, and said, Lord, how oft shall my brother sin against me, and I forgive him? till seven times? Jesus saith unto him, I say not unto thee, Until seven times: but, Until seventy times seven," (Matthew 18:21-22).

Forgive seventy times seven. Give them enough time. *Nothing Is Ever As It First Appears.* Things are happening you cannot see. Sometimes it takes weeks and even months for some to realize and admit their mistakes.

Give them a *Season of Solitude.*

Give them *Opportunities for Expression,* and an Opportunity to Explain themselves. They may not know the right choice of words the first time. *Be willing to listen longer.*

Give them a *Season for Evaluation...of every part* of the puzzle. You may be looking at one part. They are considering many different factors they have yet to discuss with you.

Give them time to *discover* the truth about you. You already know yourself. *They do not.* They do not know all of your flaws. They do not know all of your capabilities. They do not understand your memories...your pain...your goals or dreams.

Those Without Your Memories Cannot Feel Your Pain.

They may be looking at *now.*

You are looking at *tomorrow.*

Give Those Who Fail A Chance To Try Again.

This is one of the secrets to becoming an Uncommon Achiever.

DECISION

DR. MIKE MURDOCK

Will You Accept Jesus As Your Personal Savior Today?

The Bible says, "That if thou shalt confess with thy mouth the Lord Jesus, and shalt believe in thine heart that God hath raised Him from the dead, thou shalt be saved," (Romans 10:9).

Pray this prayer from your heart today!

"Dear Jesus, I believe that You died for me and rose again on the third day. I confess I am a sinner...I need Your love and forgiveness...Come into my heart. Forgive my sins. I receive Your eternal life. Confirm Your love by giving me peace, joy and supernatural love for others. Amen."

DR. MIKE MURDOCK is in tremendous demand as one of the most dynamic speakers in America today.

More than 16,000 audiences in 39 countries have attended his Schools of Wisdom and Conferences. Hundreds of invitations come to him from churches, colleges and business corporations. He is a noted author of over 200 books, including the best sellers, *The Leadership Secrets of Jesus* and *Secrets of the Richest Man Who Ever Lived.* Thousands view his weekly television program, *Wisdom Keys with Mike Murdock.* Many have attended his Schools of Wisdom that he hosts in many cities of America.

❑ Yes, Mike! I made a decision to accept Christ as my personal Savior today. Please send me my free gift of your book, *31 Keys to a New Beginning* to help me with my new life in Christ.

NAME _____ BIRTHDATE _____

ADDRESS _____

CITY _____ STATE _____ ZIP _____

PHONE _____ E-MAIL _____

Mail To:
The Wisdom Center · 4051 Denton Hwy. · Ft. Worth, TX 76117
1-817-759-BOOK · 1-817-759-0300
You Will Love Our Website: TheWisdomCenter.tv

Clip and Mail

Wisdom Key 3000

TODAY!

Will You Become My Ministry Partner In The Work Of God?

Dear Friend,

God has connected us!

I have asked The Holy Spirit for 3000 Special Partners who will plant a monthly Seed of $58.00 to help me bring the gospel around the world. (58 represents 58 kinds of blessings in the Bible.)

Will you become my monthly Faith Partner in The Wisdom Key 3000? Your monthly Seed of $58.00 is so powerful in helping heal broken lives. When you sow into the work of God, 4 Miracle Harvests are guaranteed in Scripture, Isaiah 58...

▸ Uncommon Health (Isaiah 58)

▸ Uncommon Wisdom For Decision-Making (Isaiah 58)

▸ Uncommon Financial Favor (Isaiah 58)

▸ Uncommon Family Restoration (Isaiah 58)

Your Faith Partner,

Mike Murdock

P.S. Please clip the coupon attached and return it to me today, so I can rush the Wisdom Key Partnership Pak to you...or call me at 1-817-759-0300.

- -

☐ *Yes Mike, I want to join The Wisdom Key 3000.*
   Please rush The Wisdom Key Partnership Pak to me today!
☐ *Enclosed is my first monthly Seed-Faith Promise of:*
   ☐ *$58* ☐ *Other $_____.*

☐ CHECK   ☐ MONEY ORDER   ☐ AMEX   ☐ DISCOVER   ☐ MASTERCARD   ☐ VISA

Credit Card # _____ Exp. ____/____

Signature _____

Name _____ Birth Date ___/___/___

Address _____

City _____ State _____ Zip _____

Phone _____ E-Mail _____

Your Seed-Faith offerings are used to support The Wisdom Center and all its programs. Your transaction
may be electronically deposited. The Wisdom Center reserves the right to redirect funds as needed in
order to carry out our charitable purpose.

THE WISDOM CENTER 1-817-759-BOOK
4051 Denton Highway • Fort Worth, TX 76117   1-817-759-0300

— You Will Love Our Website: —
www.TheWisdomCenter.tv

It Could Happen

61 Year Old Husband's Salvation...!

I sent you $58—for my husband's salvation. He is 61 years old and has always been very grouchy and miserable all his life—sure enough! He's gotten saved and is now the softest, most gentle man.

S. - Daytona Beach, FL

Entire Family Receives Miracles From $58 Seed...!

I was fasting and praying and watching Christian TV. I flipped to an Orlando channel and saw you. The Lord used you that day to stir my faith and change my life. I was one of the 300 you called for to plant a $58 Seed for 12 months.

Since that time, I have received so many blessings:

1) Unity in my marriage.

2) My husband found a great job at a great salary — he had been unemployed for two months.

3) My brother found a job — he had not held a job in three years.

4) My niece received a $600 scholarship "out of the blue."

All of these are people who I listed as part of the 12 you said we should plant the Seed for. Before I had even paid the money, the miracles started happening...

A. - Orlando, FL

New Job On 58th Day...!

I planted a $58 Seed for my husband to get a job...J. started working — the 58th day! Glory to God!! Thank you for your teaching.

L. - Maywood, IL

To You!

Promotion With Double Pay...!

Less than 58 days ago, I sowed a $58 Seed for finances. Always within 58 days God does something. Yesterday, I was offered a promotion at work which will double my weekly pay. This promotion is for sure "a desire of my heart."
D. - Dallas, TX

96% Of Hospital Bills Paid Off...!

I planted a $58 Seed.

Two weeks ago, God proved He was faithful. We had accumulated a little over $4,000 in bills at a local hospital. To make a long story short, I received a call two days later, telling me they had been able to write off 96% of our bill, which has left a balance of $163!
D. - Lima, OH

$4,600 Raise...!

I wanted to praise God for you and the revelation about the "Covenant of 58 Blessings" and the $58 Seed. I attended your Tampa conference in May. I planted a $58 Seed at that time and also stood for your prayer for those who did not have $1,000 to plant for the new Training Center, but who would give $1,000 if God provided it. I am praising the Lord because today I received the news from my boss that I am getting a promotion in conjunction with a $4,600 raise! July 17 would be 58 days, so the Harvest came in before the end of the 58 days! So I will be able to sow that $1,000 Seed for the Training Center.
D. - Lakeland, FL

CHAMPIONS 4
Book Pak!

1. **Secrets of The Journey, Vol. 3** /<u>Book</u> (32pg/B-94/$5)
2. **My Personal Dream Book**/<u>Book</u> (32pg/B-143/$5)
3. **Wisdom For Crisis Times** /<u>Book</u> (112pg/B-40/$9)
4. **The Making Of A Champion** /<u>Book</u> (128pg/B-59/$10)

The Wisdom Center
Champions 4 Book Pak!
Only $**20** $29 Value
PAK-23
Wisdom Is The Principal Thing

Each Wisdom Book may be purchased separately if so desired.

Add 10% For S/H

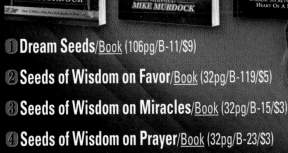

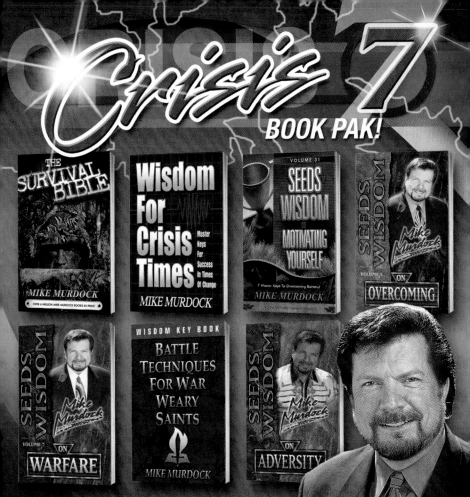

Crisis 7 BOOK PAK!

1. **The Survival Bible**/Book (248pg/B-29/$10)
2. **Wisdom For Crisis Times**/Book (112pg/B-40/$9)
3. **Seeds of Wisdom on Motivating Yourself**/Book (32pg/B-171/$5)
4. **Seeds of Wisdom on Overcoming**/Book (32pg/B-17/$3)
5. **Seeds of Wisdom on Warfare**/Book (32pg/B-19/$3)
6. **Battle Techniques For War-Weary Saints**/Book (32pg/B-07/$5)
7. **Seeds of Wisdom on Adversity**/Book (32pg/B-21/$3)

DR. MIKE MURDOCK

The Wisdom Center
Crisis 7 Book Pak!
Only $30 $38 Value
WBL-25
Wisdom Is The Principal Thing

Add 10% For S/H

Quantity Prices Available Upon Request

**Each Wisdom Book may be purchased separately if so desired.

THE WISDOM CENTER
4051 Denton Highway • Fort Worth, TX 76117
1-817-759-BOOK
1-817-759-0300

You Will Love Our Website...!
TheWisdomCenter.tv

C

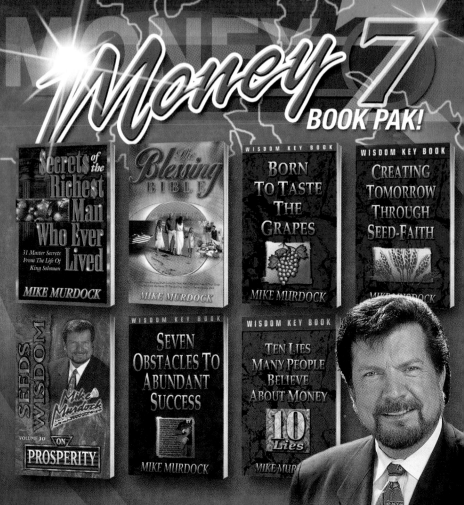

Money 7 BOOK PAK!

1. **Secrets of the Richest Man Who Ever Lived**/<u>Book</u> (179pg/B-99/$10)
2. **The Blessing Bible**/<u>Book</u> (252pg/B-28/$10)
3. **Born To Taste The Grapes**/<u>Book</u> (32pg/B-65/$3)
4. **Creating Tomorrow Through Seed-Faith**/<u>Book</u> (32pg/B-06/$5)
5. **Seeds of Wisdom on Prosperity**/<u>Book</u> (32pg/B-22/$3)
6. **Seven Obstacles To Abundant Success**/<u>Book</u> (32pg/B-64/$3)
7. **Ten Lies Many People Believe About Money**/<u>Book</u> (32pg/B-04/$5)

DR. MIKE MURDOCK

The Wisdom Center
Money 7 Book Pak!
Only $**30** $39 Value
WBL-30
Wisdom Is The Principal Thing

Add 10% For S/H

**Each Wisdom Book may be purchased separately if so desired.

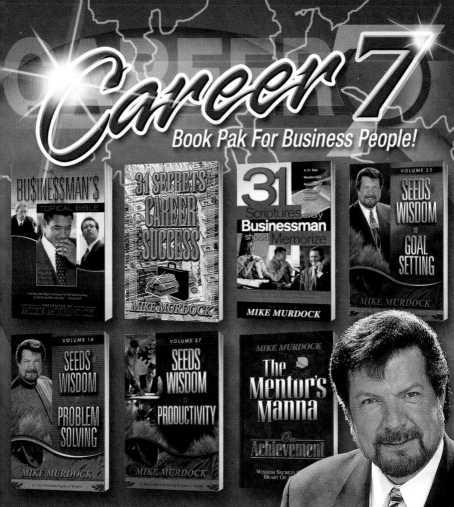

Career 7
Book Pak For Business People!

DR. MIKE MURDOCK

1. **The Businessman's Topical Bible**/<u>Book</u> (384pg/B-33/$10)

2. **31 Secrets for Career Success**/<u>Book</u> (114pg/B-44/$10)

3. **31 Scriptures Every Businessman Should Memorize**/<u>Book</u> (32pg/B-141/$3)

4. **Seeds of Wisdom on Goal-Setting**/<u>Book</u> (32pg/B-127/$5)

5. **Seeds of Wisdom on Problem-Solving**/<u>Book</u> (32pg/B-118/$5)

6. **Seeds of Wisdom on Productivity**/<u>Book</u> (32pg/B-137/$5)

7. **The Mentor's Manna on Achievement**/<u>Book</u> (32pg/B-79/$3)

**Each Wisdom Book may be purchased separately if so desired.

The Wisdom Center
Career 7 Book Pak!
Only $30 $41 Value
WBL-27
Wisdom Is The Principal Thing

Add 10% For S/H

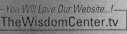

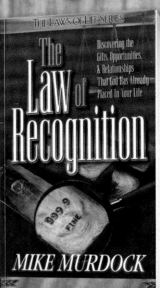

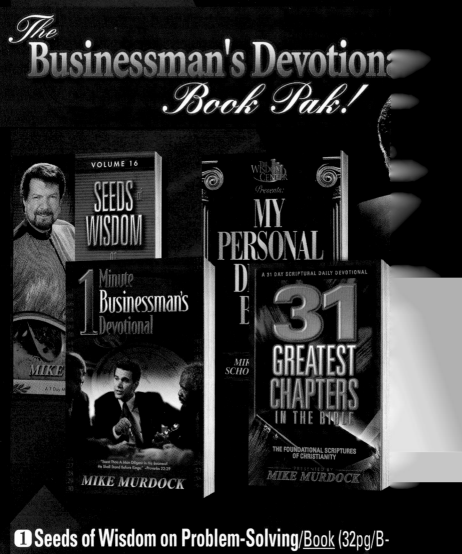

The Businessman's Devotional Book Pak!

VOLUME 16
SEEDS OF WISDOM

1 Minute Businessman's Devotional

"Seest Thou A Man Diligent In His Business? He Shall Stand Before Kings." -Proverbs 22:29

MIKE MURDOCK

THE WISDOM CENTER Presents: MY PERSONAL D...

A 31 DAY SCRIPTURAL DAILY DEVOTIONAL
31 GREATEST CHAPTERS IN THE BIBLE
THE FOUNDATIONAL SCRIPTURES OF CHRISTIANITY
PRESENTED BY **MIKE MURDOCK**

❶ **Seeds of Wisdom on Problem-Solving**/<u>Book</u> (32pg/B-

❷ **My Personal Dream Book**/<u>Book</u> (32pg/B-143/$5)

❸ **1 Minute Businessman's Devotional**
/<u>Book</u> (224pg/B-42/$12)

❹ **31 Greatest Chapters In The Bible**
/<u>Book</u> (138pg/B-54/$10)

**Each Wisdom Book may be purchased separately if so desired.

The Wisdo
Th
Businessma
tional 4 B
Only **$2**
Wisdom Is The
PAK

Add 10%

THE TURNAROUND Collection

THE *Mike Murdock* COLLECTOR'S EDITION

THE Wisdom COMMENTARY 1

WISDOM KEY BOOK

BATTLE TECHNIQUES FOR WAR WEARY SAINTS

MIKE MURDOCK

SEEDS of WISDOM

VOLUME 5

Mike Murdock

ON OVERCOMING

Volume 2

The Memory Bible on Healing

PRESENTED BY MIKE MURDOCK

WISDOM KEY BOOK

HOW TO TURN YOUR MISTAKES INTO MIRACLES

MIKE MURDOCK

THE MIKE MURDOCK Partnership Library

7 Keys To Turning Your Life Around

FREE BOOK ENCLOSED!

VOL 3 UME

THE MIKE MURDOCK Music Library

FREE BOOK ENCLOSED!

VOL 1 UME

The Sun Will Shine Again

❶ The Wisdom Commentary Vol. 1/Book (256pg/52 Topics/B-136/$20)

❷ Battle Techniques For War-Weary Saints/Book (32pg/B-07/$5)

❸ Seeds of Wisdom on Overcoming/Book (32pg/B-17/$3)

❹ The Memory Bible on Healing/Book (32pg/B-196/$3)

❺ How To Turn Your Mistakes Into Miracles/Book (32pg/B-56/$5)

❻ 7 Keys To Turning Your Life Around/DVD (MMPL-03D/$10)

❼ The Sun Will Shine Again/Music CD (MMML-01/$10)

The Wisdom Center
Celebrating
40 Years of
Global Ministry!
Wisdom Is The Principal Thing

The Wisdom Center
The
Turnaround Collection
Only $40 $56 Value
PAK-15
Wisdom Is The Principal Thing

Add 10% For S/H

**Each Wisdom Product may be purchased separately if so desired.*

Favor 4!

THE SCHOOL of WISDOM
31 KEYS TO UNLEASHING UNCOMMON FAVOR
MIKE MURDOCK

Pastoral Collection of Mike Murdock
The Hidden Power Of Right Words

SEEDS of WISDOM on FAVOR
MIKE MURDOCK

SEEDS of WISDOM on OBEDIENCE

This Collection Of Wisdom Will Change The Seasons Of Your Life Forever!

1. The School of Wisdom #4 / 31 Keys To Unleashing Uncommon Favor...Tape Series/6 Cassettes (TS-44/S30)

2. The Hidden Power Of Right Words... The Wisdom Center Pastoral Library/CD (WCPL-27/S10)

3. Seeds of Wisdom on Favor/Book (32pg/B-119/S5)

4. Seeds of Wisdom on Obedience/Book (32pg/B-20/S3)

The Wisdom Center
Favor 4 Collection!
Only $35 $48 Value
PAK-12
Wisdom Is The Principal Thing

Add 10% For S/H

**Each Wisdom Product may be purchased separately if so desired.

Financial $ecrets.

THE 31 DAY MENTORSHIP PROGRAM

31 REASONS
PEOPLE DO NOT RECEIVE THEIR
FINANCIAL HARVEST
MIKE MURDOCK

VIDEO

7 KEYS TO 1000 TIMES MORE
The Lord God Of Your Fathers Make You A Thousand Times So Many More As You Are And Bless You, As He Hath Promised You!
Deuteronomy 1:11
MIKE MURDOCK

Your Financial World Will Change Forever.

Video 2-Pak!

▸ 8 Scriptural Reasons You Should Pursue Financial Prosperity

▸ The Secret Prayer Key You Need When Making A Financial Request To God

▸ The Weapon Of Expectation And The 5 Miracles It Unlocks

▸ How To Discern Those Who Qualify To Receive Your Financial Assistance

▸ How To Predict The Miracle Moment God Will Schedule Your Financial Breakthrough

▸ Habits Of Uncommon Achievers

▸ The Greatest Success Law I Ever Discovered

▸ How To Discern Your Place Of Assignment, The Only Place Financial Provision Is Guaranteed

▸ 3 Secret Keys In Solving Problems For Others

**Each Wisdom Product may be purchased separately if so desired.

THE WISDOM BIBLE

Partnership Edition

Over 120 Wisdom Study Guides Included Such As:

- 10 Qualities Of Uncommon Achievers
- 18 Facts You Should Know About The Anointing
- 21 Facts To Help You Identify Those Assigned To You
- 31 Facts You Should Know About Your Assignment
- 8 Keys That Unlock Victory In Every Attack
- 22 Defense Techniques To Remember During Seasons Of Personal Attack
- 20 Wisdom Keys And Techniques To Remember During An Uncommon Battle
- 11 Benefits You Can Expect From God
- 31 Facts You Should Know About Favor
- The Covenant Of 58 Blessings
- 7 Keys To Receiving Your Miracle
- 16 Facts You Should Remember About Contentious People
- 5 Facts Solomon Taught About Contracts
- 7 Facts You Should Know About Conflict
- 6 Steps That Can Unlock Your Self-Confidence
- And Much More!

Your Partnership makes such a difference in The Wisdom Center Outreach Ministries. I wanted to place a Gift in your hand that could last a lifetime for you and your family...**The Wisdom Study Bible.**

40 Years of Personal Notes...this Partnership Edition Bible contains 160 pages of my Personal Study Notes...that could forever change your Bible Study of The Word of God. This **Partnership Edition...**is my personal **Gift of Appreciation** when you sow your Sponsorship Seed of $1,000 to help us complete The Prayer Center and TV Studio Complex. An Uncommon Seed Always Creates An Uncommon Harvest!

Mike

Thank you from my heart for your Seed of Obedience (Luke 6:38).

Spirit Music.

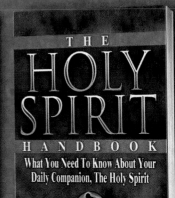

The Mike Murdock Music Library

LOVE SONGS TO THE HOLY SPIRIT

Written In The Secret Place

TS-59

LOVE SONGS TO THE HOLY SPIRIT

DR. MIKE MURDOCK

THE HOLY SPIRIT HANDBOOK

What You Need To Know About Your Daily Companion, The Holy Spirit

The Wisdom Center
Free Book ENCLOSED!
B-100 ($10 Value)
Wisdom Is The Principal Thing

Songs...

1. A Holy Place
2. Anything You Want
3. Everything Comes From You
4. Fill This Place With Your Presence
5. First Thing Every Morning
6. Holy Spirit, I Want To Hear You
7. Holy Spirit, Move Again
8. Holy Spirit, You Are Enough
9. I Don't Know What I Would Do Without You
10. I Let Go (Of Anything That Stops Me)
11. I'll Just Fall On You
12. I Love You, Holy Spirit
13. I'm Building My Life Around You
14. I'm Giving Myself To You
15. I'm In Love! I'm In Love!
16. I Need Water (Holy Spirit, You're My Well)
17. In The Secret Place

18. In Your Presence, I'm Always Changed
19. In Your Presence (Miracles Are Born)
20. I've Got To Live In Your Presence
21. I Want To Hear Your Voice
22. I Will Do Things Your Way
23. Just One Day At A Time
24. Meet Me In The Secret Place
25. More Than Ever Before
26. Nobody Else Does What You Do
27. No No Walls!
28. Nothing Else Matters Anymore (Since I've Been In The Presence Of You Lord)
29. Nowhere Else
30. Once Again You've Answered
31. Only A Fool Would Try (To Live Without You)
32. Take Me Now
33. Teach Me How To Please You

34. There's No Place I'd Rather Be
35. Thy Word Is All That Matters
36. When I Get In Your Presence
37. You're The Best Thing (That's Ever Happened To Me)
38. You Are Wonderful
39. You've Done It Once
40. You Keep Changing Me
41. You Satisfy

The Wisdom Center
6 Tapes/Only $30*
PAK007
Wisdom Is The Principal Thing

Add 10% For S/H

DISCOVER MasterCard VISA

*Each Wisdom Product may be purchased separately if so desired.

THE WISDOM CENTER · 4051 Denton Highway • Fort Worth, TX 76117

1-817-759-BOOK
1-817-759-0300

You Will Love Our Website...!
TheWisdomCenter.tv

N